TREND FORECASTING

With

INTERMARKET ANALYSIS

PREDICTING GLOBAL MARKETS WITH TECHNICAL ANALYSIS

2ND EDITION

TREND FORECASTING

With

INTERMARKET ANALYSIS

PREDICTING GLOBAL MARKETS WITH TECHNICAL ANALYSIS

2ND EDITION

LOUIS B. MENDELSOHN
FOREWORD BY JIM WYCKOFF

WILEY

John Wiley & Sons, Inc.

TRA

SEC

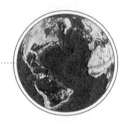

For general information about our other products and services, please contact our
Customer Care Department within the United States at (800) 762-2974, outside the
United States at (317) 572-3993 or fax (317) 572-4002.

Wiley publishes in a variety of print and electronic formats and by print-on-demand.
Some material included with standard print versions of this book may not be included in
e-books or in print-on-demand. If this book refers to media such as a CD or DVD
that is not included in the version you purchased, you may download this material
at http://booksupport.wiley.com. For more information about Wiley products, visit
www.wiley.com.

ISBN 978-1-592-80332-3

Printed in the United States of America

10 9 8 7 6 5 4 3 2

CONTENTS

FOREWORD

I HAVE BEEN involved in markets and trading for nearly a quarter century. Starting out as a journalist on the trading floors of the futures exchanges in Chicago and New York was an excellent way for me to begin to learn about "the ways of the markets."

Being able to walk right up to floor traders in the trading pits, on a daily basis, and ask them all kinds of questions about markets and price action was an excellent—and rare—opportunity to learn the ropes. I took full advantage of that opportunity as a floor reporter on the exchanges, including attending as many trading seminars and workshops as my editors would allow.

Not long after beginning my career on the rough-and-tumble futures trading floors, I realized that the floor traders often did have an edge over most retail traders in the futures markets because they were eyeball-to-eyeball with other traders and could see firsthand who was buying and who was selling. After all, they were filling orders for some of the biggest and best traders in the world. But those who traded for their own accounts had another advantage: They relied mainly on technical analysis to provide them with early clues about imminent trending price moves.

Because technical analysis takes into account all the fundamental news that has or is expected to occur in a market, as reflected by the most recent price activity, these traders could see price patterns and movements that provided them with a roadmap for trading profits. To put it another way, if a trader decided to rely only upon fundamental analysis to analyze and trade markets, he or she would spend nearly all of his or her day studying past and present news events and supply and demand statistics, only to have all that information already digested by and factored into the market price structure.

Today's trading world is going more and more electronic, diminishing the importance of the face-to-face confrontations in the open-outcry pits. And with electronic trading and advances in communications technologies, markets have gotten increasingly more global, with factors that affect one market influencing what happens in other markets. Traders can no longer do a market-by-market analysis without considering what is happening in related markets. Technical analysis needs to adapt to global conditions.

When respected veteran trader and trading software developer Louis Mendelsohn came to that realization more than two decades ago, he started to take technical analysis one step—or two or three steps—further. For more than 20 years he has advocated and developed an "intermarket" approach to market analysis and trading. Intermarket analysis theory (actually, trading professionals know it as fact) suggests that all markets are interrelated and behave in ways and patterns that are based upon other markets' price behavior.

I know intermarket analysis as fact and can illustrate it with several compelling examples. The first occurred very early in my career as a financial market journalist. I covered several markets a day while reporting on the trading floor for what is now the Dow Jones Newswires service. Among the markets I covered were stock index futures. In doing my pre-opening market call for stock indexes, I would ask floor traders about the likely price direction for the day. Nearly every day the response I'd get from the stock index traders would be, "Well, based upon what the bonds are doing in early trading, we expect the stock indexes to . . . ."

And when I covered the grains, the pre-opening calls invariably would be based partly upon what the U.S. dollar, stock indexes, and precious metals had done in overnight trading. The same type of intermarket relationships was evident when I covered the precious metals, where traders looked to the value of the U.S. dollar for direction.

More recently, there has been a defining example of the reality of intermarket behavior in what I have termed the "axis" markets: crude oil, gold, and the U.S. dollar versus the other major currencies. Because crude oil and gold are priced in dollars, those who produce these commodities are getting more paper but less value for their products when the dollar weakens, as was highlighted in many media reports about nations shifting or threatening to shift their currency reserves into euros or something other than dollars. In many cases, if the price of oil goes up, so does the price of gold while the value of the dollar declines, although the intermarket relationships aren't quite that simplistic.

These three markets combined have a powerful influence on daily price activity in grains and many other commodity markets. In fact, for a while the axis markets were the main factor driving prices.

Then, of course, there has been the impact on many markets from issues related to the sub-prime mortgage debacle, which seems to have stretched its tentacles everywhere. Losses from these loans and the decreasing credit liquidity as banks tighten their lending policies have prompted government and Federal Reserve responses that have affected interest rates, stock indexes, currencies, and virtually every other financial market. The effect hasn't been limited to U.S. financial firms but has had repercussions globally almost from the first day that the situation began to deteriorate.

Imagine the trading advantage you could enjoy if you could quantify the relationships among markets and employ intermarket analysis in the markets you trade when these types of developments surface. Since the early 1980s, this has been the thrust of Mendelsohn's ongoing quest; he is a pioneer in applying the personal computer to trading futures markets and developing intermarket analysis software.

This book explains how his solution for intermarket analysis, VantagePoint Intermarket Analysis Software, can be used as a powerful trading tool when combined with fundamentals and traditional technical analysis in what Louis Mendelsohn calls a "synergistic trading approach." His work and research isn't done yet, but he continues to be at the forefront of technical analysis by developing new and unique indicators and applying them to an expanding number of world markets.

Jim Wyckoff

Senior Market Analyst
www.TraderPlanet.com

PREFACE

INTERMARKET ANALYSIS is the analysis of the relationships between financial markets and their influences on each other; this book explores the application of this process to trading in today's global economy. It examines the role that intermarket analysis plays in helping traders to identify and forecast changes in trend directions and prices, in view of the unprecedented extent to which global financial markets have become interconnected and interdependent.

These include the relationships of stock indices such as the S&P 500 Index, the Nasdaq 100 Index, and the FTSE 100; gold; currencies such as the U.S. Dollar Index, Euro, British Pound, and Japanese Yen; energy markets such as crude oil, heating oil, and gasoline; interest rate markets such as Treasury Notes and Bonds; and individual equities.

As the burgeoning world economy of the 21st century has contributed to the further globalization of the financial markets (fostered by advancements in information technologies), intermarket analysis has become a critical facet of the overall field of technical analysis. Intermarket analysis empowers individual traders to make more effective trading decisions based upon the linkages between related financial markets. By incorporating intermarket analysis into your trading plans and strategies, instead of limiting your scope of analysis to each individual market in isolation, you can make these relationships and interconnections between markets work for you, instead of against you.

This book makes suggestions for how leading indicators, created through the application of intermarket analysis, can be used in conjunction with traditional single-market technical analysis indicators to provide a broadened perspective and framework of analysis for trading. This allows traders to make more effective and decisive trading decisions than would be possible by relying on traditional single-market technical analysis indicators that too often lag the market.

Offering insights into how day traders and position traders in both the equities and futures markets can improve their trading performance and achieve a competitive advantage in today's globally interdependent financial markets, this book is addressed primarily to traders and investors who utilize personal computers and the Internet to analyze various financial markets and make their own trading decisions. The book does not attempt to give an in-depth presentation on popular technical analysis indicators, nor does it detail the underlying mathematics behind the intermarket analysis methods and strategies that are discussed.

This book will be of interest to both experienced traders and newcomers to the financial markets who are inclined toward technical analysis and intent on participating in the wealth creation of today's global financial markets by incorporating intermarket analysis tools into their trading strategies.

INTRODUCTION

I AM VERY fortunate to have been involved in the field of technical analysis for more than 35 years and to have played a prominent role as the events surrounding the early application of personal computers to the financial markets began to unfold, and after PCs first appeared on the scene.

In the early 1970s, while studying for a M.S.W. degree in Buffalo, New York, I began trading stocks and options as a hobby, using various popular technical analysis methods. Initially, I subscribed to weekly chart services, which had to be updated by hand during the week, requiring a sharp pencil to draw support and resistance lines.

Several years later after working as a regional health planner, I enrolled in the MBA program at Boston University with an emphasis on health care management. Interestingly, I spent most of my free time at B.U. studying technical analysis and playing the stock market, although I still managed to get my MBA degree with Honors and looked forward to a career in hospital administration. During that time I also met and married my wife, Illyce.

In the years before the advent of personal computers, with only a handheld calculator available to compute numbers, I familiarized myself with the underlying theories and mathematical equations for numerous technical indicators, and devised mathematical shortcuts to expedite my daily calculations and to cut down on errors.

After relocating to south Florida to work for Humana as a hospital administrator in 1977, I read an interesting article in the *Wall Street Journal* about personal computers, which at the time were called "microcomputers." That evening I drove to a nearby Radio Shack to see one firsthand. I was already quite proficient with my Texas Instruments handheld calculator and familiar with IBM mainframe computers from my undergraduate college days at Carnegie Mellon in the 1960s, but having a desktop computer and being able to write and execute programs on the spot was a whole different experience.

When I walked out of the store to my car, I had an "ah-ha" moment: I thought to myself that the world is about to undergo a profound change due to this new invention, and I was excited as I contemplated how I could apply this new technology to technical analysis and my own trading.

Shortly afterwards, I was promoted by Humana to become the Assistant Executive Director of another one of its hospitals in Tampa, Florida, and soon developed a personal friendship with a pathologist there who was trading commodity futures at the time. This was during the inflationary period when interest rates and gold prices were skyrocketing, and a $1 million T-bill contract could be controlled with as little as $1,000 margin. So, there was an incredible buzz surrounding commodities trading—and I caught the bug. At that point I re-directed my focus and began trading commodities exclusively as both a day and position trader—all while managing a hospital.

On evenings and weekends I taught myself a programming language called Basic and started writing trading software programs to automate various technical analysis indicators that I previously had been calculating by hand. It didn't take long for me to realize that trading software would dramatically change technical analysis and richly reward software developers who understood the financial markets from a trader's perspective and could program that knowledge into trading software.

Although I had been hooked on technical analysis for nearly a decade by then, and found commodities trading practically addictive, it was the challenge of applying personal computers and software to technical analysis, more so than trading itself, which crystallized the intellectual and entrepreneurial passion that I had sought but never found in the health care industry.

In 1979, at 31 years old and intent on pursuing my passion, I started a trading software company that, through several name changes over the decades, became known as Market Technologies. I was determined to develop trading software that would revolutionize technical analysis. A year later, just after our first son, Lane, was born and with Illyce's encouragement and her income from a tutoring agency that she had started in Tampa, I left Humana and hospital administration to devote my full attention to developing trading software and trading on a full-time basis.

Working alone and at a near-feverish pace, I literally spent day and night for the next few years researching the commodities futures markets, studying more sophisticated aspects of technical analysis, and examining my winning and losing trades for patterns to incorporate into my evolving trading strategies. Most importantly, I continued to develop and refine trading software for my own use and ultimately to license to other commodities traders who, I believed, would be hungry for trading software to help them make more effective and profitable trading decisions.

In 1983, after three years of nearly "solitary confinement," I completed my first trading software program that I felt proud enough to share with other commodities traders and began licensing it under the name ProfitTaker Futures Trading software.

I received personal encouragement from several already-prominent technical analysts and commodities traders with whom I shared my ideas about the strategy back-testing capabilities that I had incorporated into ProfitTaker. Foremost among these individuals was Darrell Jobman, who at the time was the editor of *Futures* magazine. He recognized the significance of applying this new technology of personal computers and trading software to the financial markets and published a series of my articles in *Futures*. In these articles I introduced the concept of strategy back-testing and optimization for personal computers and detailed the impact that I thought back-testing would have on the conduct of technical analysis.

Almost immediately upon its release, ProfitTaker was recognized in the financial industry as the first commercially available strategy back-testing and optimization trading software for personal computers. This was a momentous year in which my wife and I celebrated both the birth of our second son, Ean, and that of ProfitTaker.

During the next few years I introduced new, more powerful versions of ProfitTaker, wrote more articles on technical analysis in various trading publications, collaborated on several books on technical analysis, and gave presentations at industry conferences. I spoke about the application of personal computers to trading and warned about the pitfalls of curve-fitting and over-optimization in the design and testing of trading strategies.

In early 1986, while running my software company and recovering from a car accident, I started noticing subtle changes taking place in the markets that seemed to involve their interaction with one another in a way that, I believed, if quantified, could prove useful in identifying and forecasting trend changes. This, I concluded, would eventually help traders make better trading decisions, and ultimately more money.

I attributed these changes in market dynamics to advances that were occurring in both computing and telecommunications technologies worldwide, which tended to bring the world's previously distinct financial markets closer together. I didn't know at the time that this emerging phenomenon that had piqued my interest would come to be referred to as the "global economy" years later.

It was becoming increasingly apparent to me that the prevailing approach to trading software, in which each market is analyzed by itself in terms of its internal dynamics by using trend-following, lagging indicators (such as ProfitTaker's), might become outdated. I concluded that this market-by-market focus, which had been the mainstay of technical analysis for decades, would no longer be sufficient in the future.

Because I had previously pioneered strategy back-testing for personal computers, and thrived on staying at the cutting-edge of trading software development, I felt that it was imperative for me to push trading software to the next generation. I wanted to introduce a whole new approach to technical analysis that would look at the markets from a broader perspective.

My goal was to quantify the links between related financial markets and to use this "intermarket" information to make accurate forecasts of market trends. This would allow traders to make more effective and timely trading decisions than could be done with the narrow, single-market approach that still dominated the trading software industry, which, by then, had begun to mature as more competitors entered the field.

By late 1986, I had developed a working prototype of what would become my second trading software program, which focused on market interdependencies. The program, which I named Trader, later gained recognition as the first commercially available intermarket analysis trading software for PCs in the financial industry. It used a spreadsheet format to correlate the expected trend direction of a target market with those of related markets, as well as with expectations regarding various fundamental economic indicators affecting each target market.

Despite these early efforts at performing intermarket analysis that went beyond simple ratios of, or differences between, markets or commodity contract months, I was not satisfied with the underlying mathematical rigor used to correlate intermarket data in the Trader program and felt compelled to continue my search for a more robust mathematical tool.

As the forces behind the globalization of the financial markets continued to gain strength, as evidenced by the global stock market crash of October 1987, I was sure that technical analysis was on the verge of a total transformation in scope. I concluded that the interdependencies of the world's equities, futures, and derivatives markets would necessitate the inclusion of an intermarket perspective, and I was determined to find a more precise way to quantify these intermarket relationships in software. I was particularly desirous of being able to do so from a multi-market perspective in which the software could handle multiple markets simultaneously affecting a given target market.

Subsequently, in the late 1980s, while my wife and I were dealing with severe medical problems that our third son, Lee, had at birth, I continued to investigate and apply various ways to quantify intermarket relationships. While our son underwent several surgeries at Children's

Hospital in Pittsburgh over the following two years, I began experimenting with a mathematical tool called neural networks, which is a form of "artificial intelligence." I remembered this vaguely from academic material I reviewed while an undergraduate at Carnegie Mellon University in the late 1960s. A professor there, Herbert A. Simon, was an early pioneer in the field of artificial intelligence and its application to decision-making under conditions of uncertainty.

In neural networks I found the right tool for the job! Through my research, I was able to quantify multiple intermarket relationships and find hidden patterns between related markets that were increasingly responsible for price movements in the emerging global economy of the late 1980s.

In 1991, I began licensing my second-generation intermarket analysis trading software program to commodities traders. This program applied neural networks to intermarket data. I named the program VantagePoint Intermarket Analysis Software because I felt that intermarket analysis would afford traders a broader "vantage point" on the markets than could be achieved by analyzing individual markets by themselves. At first VantagePoint only dealt with the 30-year Treasury Bond. The following year I added several currencies.

By the 1990s strategy back-testing had become the backbone of single-market technical analysis software being sold throughout the world. To the huge influx of new traders during the dot com boom (who were just learning the basics of technical analysis through their first exposure to trading software), it must have seemed as if back-testing had always existed in software. These traders didn't have the faintest clue about the evolution of trading software since the advent of personal computers, which is understandable. But, more importantly, they had little or no appreciation for the growing interdependencies between global markets and the need to incorporate an intermarket perspective into their trading strategies.

Throughout the remainder of the 1990s and early 2000s, I have continued to oversee all aspects of Market Technologies, which has grown considerably in size and now has trading software customers in more than 90 countries. Beginning in 2004, the research and development efforts on VantagePoint were increased substantially as the Predictive Technologies Group, which is responsible for R&D, added forex, ETFs, and individual stocks to the commodities markets already covered, continued to refine the neural networks' predictive accuracy, and incorporated new predictive indicators into VantagePoint. Now, more than 15 years since VantagePoint was first released, the current version uses advanced neural networks to analyze intermarket data on literally hundreds of global financial markets each day.

Both Lane and Ean share my passion for the financial markets and technical analysis in their own ways. Since they were both very young children, they have accompanied me to numerous industry conferences and seminars, where they have gotten to know many prominent technical analysts and traders. They have also contributed over the years to the growth and success of Market Technologies.

Ean's involvement, starting when he was just 13 years old, has been focused mostly on expanding and supporting VantagePoint's customer base, while Lane's interests have been broader in scope and include marketing as well as R&D. At 15 he developed our first corporate website. More recently, Lane's attention has primarily been on educating traders about the financial markets as founder and Publisher of TraderPlanet.com, which is a free, advertiser-supported, educational and social networking website for traders.

I am happy to say that Darrell Jobman is still very active in the financial industry and over the years has become a close personal friend. As Editor-in-Chief of www.TraderPlanet.com, he oversees all of its educational content and works very closely with Lane. That leaves me with one more personal challenge—namely, figuring out how to get our youngest son, Lee, excited by the markets and involved in Market Technologies. Admittedly, he's had a rough time, most recently involving major back surgery related to his problems at birth. So, Illyce and I have cut him quite a bit of slack relative to our other two sons.

As you can see from this account of my personal and professional life over the past quarter-century, I have been focused on applying trading software to the global financial markets and mentoring our sons to follow in my entrepreneurial footsteps. I have also tried to instill my passion and interest in the financial markets and technical analysis to traders around the world through my published articles and books. I hope that this book will help to encourage others to embrace technical analysis and treat their trading in a business-like fashion and not to just look for some elusive magic bullet that simply doesn't exist.

The focus of this book is on how to apply intermarket analysis in today's global markets and how to turn lagging technical indicators into predictive, leading indicators through the application of intermarket data.

Chapter 1 discusses the globalization of the financial markets and outlines some of the major factors that are responsible for the emergence of the "Global Economy."

Chapter 2 highlights the limitations of traditional technical analysis methods, particularly the emphasis on single-market analysis and the reliance upon "lagging" trend-following technical indicators.

Chapter 3 offers background information on technical analysis, particularly chart formations as they are used for trend forecasting.

Chapter 4 examines popular technical indicators, which attempt to quantify market data for trend identification.

Chapter 5 examines intermarket analysis as a logical extension of technical analysis and discusses various ways that intermarket analysis can be used by traders to improve their trading performance.

Chapter 6 looks at the application of neural networks to intermarket analysis and briefly outlines the basics of what neural networks are and how they can benefit traders in today's global economy.

Chapter 7 looks at VantagePoint Intermarket Analysis software and shows how it applies intermarket data to create predictive technical indicators.

Chapter 8 discusses several trading strategies that can be applied using VantagePoint's predictive indicators.

Chapter 9 discusses the evolution of market analysis in the first decade of the 21st century. It highlights a comprehensive method of analysis that I call "Synergistic Market Analysis," which uses neural networks to combine technical, intermarket, and fundamental data into one framework for the purpose of trend identification and forecasting.

In summary, this book discusses the globalization of the world's financial markets and the application of intermarket analysis in developing and implementing powerful trend-forecasting and market-timing trading strategies in the equities, options, futures, and forex markets.

Chapter 1

TRADING IN A GLOBAL ECONOMY

Change is one of the constants of life. If you're a long-time trader, it's been coming at you with increasing speed in the last few decades, totally altering the landscape of the traditional open-outcry auction market that characterized trading since the middle of the 19th century.

The 1970s introduced financial futures contracts on currencies and interest rates for the first time, as well as a new energy market and the ability for U.S. investors to own gold again after a more than 40-year hiatus. Throw in a steep stock market setback and inflationary conditions that propelled prices of commodities, such as soybeans and sugar, to astronomical levels, and investors began to flock to the commodity trading arena in a big way.

The 1980s produced a number of new trading concepts and instruments—cash-settled futures contracts, options on futures, and futures and options based on stock indexes. As inflation cooled, the markets shifted from contracts based primarily on physicals to new offerings based on paper. The advent of personal computers opened up participation in these markets to a new generation of individual traders and, as personal computers advanced, software designed to analyze and trade markets proliferated as more traders turned to technical analysis techniques to help them make their trading decisions.

The 1990s brought the Internet, a quantum leap in global communications that ushered in the global economy and opened up the information world to traders. This set the stage for electronic trading, which culminated in the technology stock "bubble" that took the stock market to unprecedented levels before the "irrational exuberance" of day-traders and others caught up with the market. Right now, personal computers and analytic software continue to undergo significant improvements in speed, performance, and user-friendliness.

The 2000s built on the technological advances of the Internet and personal computers in all areas of business and daily life, perhaps most notably in the trading industry's shift to electronic trading. Within a short time after contracts became available on electronic platforms, trading volumes set records in currencies, stock indexes, and many other markets as hedge funds, loaded up with bundles of cash needing to be deployed, became dominant market players with which individual traders had to contend and compete. Electronic trading played a big role in changing the face of the financial markets and trading industry as the global economy expanded and various exchanges throughout the world merged with one another or made the transition from membership organizations to publicly owned companies.

ONE CONSTANT REMAINS

Yet, with all the advances in technology and all the resources now available to individual traders, one statistic has remained relatively constant over the years: The overall success rate of individual traders from a profitability standpoint has not improved materially since the days of pit trading. One reason, in my opinion, is that technical analysis has continued to emphasize a market-by-market approach and has not kept pace with structural changes that have occurred in the financial markets related to the emergence of the global economy. Another important reason is that individual traders often lack an adequate understanding of market behavior, dynamics, and the mechanics of trading. As a result, there is an enormous need for education and training, particularly for novice traders who are just getting involved in the global financial markets.

With the speed and extent of data and news now available, mass psychology and market sentiment seem to change daily, if not hourly. Based on the latest tidbit of information—or misinformation—market sentiment abruptly shifts from bullish to bearish and back again. One day a futures market or individual stock is overbought, the next day it is oversold. One day concerns over higher oil prices, due to a threatened hurricane's effects on oil rigs in the Gulf of Mexico and refineries on the Gulf Coast, or problems in the U.S. mortgage credit markets spreading elsewhere are of paramount importance to traders; the next day these subjects are practically forgotten as traders move on to the next hot button topic.

Just as television viewers hop from one sound bite and one hot topic to the next and switch channels with the touch of a remote control, traders have a difficult time maintaining their focus, discipline, and perspective as they try to make sense of often conflicting information about interest rates, economic growth, inflationary expectations, terrorist threats, hurricane forecasts, employment numbers, and many other day-to-day concerns and influences on the markets. To the novice, these sudden shifts between greed and fear, bullishness and bearishness, optimism and pessimism, hope and resignation, seem to take place with little rhyme or reason.

However, despite what seem like erratic and unexplainable shifts in opinions, patterns of market behavior often repeat themselves over and over again. They can be found within every market at different periods in time and by analyzing various relationships between related markets. The global financial markets now, more often than not, move in concert, driven by common financial, political and economic forces affecting the global economy.

No longer can traders rely solely upon single-market technical analysis methods, which were designed for, and more appropriate to, the relatively independent and less volatile domestic markets of the late 20th century and may have sufficed in a previous period. Intermarket analysis tools that can identify reoccurring patterns within individual financial markets and between related global markets give traders a broadened trading perspective and competitive edge in the 21st century global financial markets.

The increasing interconnectedness between financial markets, even seemingly distantly related, in the global economy and the growing interdependencies among global commodity, futures, debt and equity markets has made intermarket analysis an important and necessary facet of research and market analysis by traders. Because the markets are a financial version of Darwin's survival of the fittest competition, intermarket analysis tools and methodologies that build and expand upon single-market analysis methods demand serious attention by traders if their involvement in the financial markets is to be profitable and not just a short-lived, costly and painful learning experience.

MARKET EVOLUTION

The emergence of a new era of global electronic communications was heralded by the first transatlantic satellite transmission in 1962 and was greatly expanded by the rapid development of the Internet since the early 1990s. Together with the creation of new currency, interest rate, oil and stock index products in the 1970s and 1980s, the world's futures and equity markets, previously distinct from one another, have merged into one giant global financial network.

The proliferation of financial futures since the mid-1970s laid the early foundation for the global integration of the financial markets following the decision by the United States to abandon fixed exchange rates in 1971. Those developments have made intermarket analysis a necessary adjunct to the more traditional single-market technical analysis that proliferated following the advent of personal computers in the late 1970s, as volatility in interest and exchange rates, as well as energy prices, created new trading opportunities and risks for speculators and hedgers. This included multinational corporations and the growing number of hedge funds that scour the world's financial markets for places to put their leveraged capital to work.

In the past, trading was conducted on a local level within separate time zones on individual domestic stock and commodity exchanges. Japanese and other Far East stocks traded primarily in Tokyo or other Asian trading centers. European stocks traded in London and elsewhere in Europe. U.S. stocks traded in New York while domestic and foreign commodities and futures traded primarily in Chicago and New York. With the links between the financial centers of the world established and their influence on each other becoming more evident every day, the melding of the debt, equity, futures, derivative, and options markets throughout the world has continued unabated, most significantly in the global foreign exchange market known widely as the FX or forex market.

As these interrelationships of previously disparate markets have developed and strengthened, exchanges worldwide have been moving at a frenetic pace in the first decade of the 21st century to establish linkages with each other. Hardly a week goes by without some announcement of exchanges merging or acquiring trading partners in other areas of the world, expanding into other market arenas, or launching new electronic trading facilities. In addition, many exchanges have moved from member-owned organizations to for-profit publicly owned corporations in the last few years. It is not an exaggeration to describe these rapid changes among exchanges as a complete revolution in the trading industry, further accelerating the globalization of the financial markets.

BRAVE NEW EXCHANGE WORLD

Even the staid old exchanges of the past like the New York Stock Exchange (NYSE), Chicago Board of Trade (CBOT), and Chicago Mercantile Exchange (CME) have worked out direct ties to, or strategic alliances with, foreign exchanges. In many cases, these new arrangements between exchanges have been sparked by the drive to facilitate expanded electronic trading, which allows traders to trade any financial instrument, anywhere in the world, at any time over seamless, electronic global trading platforms.

Just look at a few of the recent new alignments in the exchange world:

- Traditional rivals like the CME and CBOT decided first to both use one clearing organization, then the CME acquired the CBOT in 2007 after a contentious battle in a merger of futures exchange leaders that surprised traders and has been hailed as the deal of the century in the trading world.

- The New York Mercantile Exchange agreed to trade its products electronically on CME's Globex platform, starting with energy and then adding metals when it became obvious that its Comex division was losing precious metals trading share to CBOT's electronically traded contracts. With the CME-CBOT merger, the CBOT metals contracts were dropped. This cooperative effort between two formerly highly competitive cities is quite a turnabout from the heated battles of the past.

- The Intercontinental Exchange (ICE), an upstart electronic energy marketplace based near Atlanta, acquired the New York Board of Trade, the last exchange to rely only on open-outcry pit trading, and changed its name to ICE Futures US in 2007. The acquisition produced an instant boost in volume in cotton, sugar, cocoa, and coffee futures when those contracts started trading electronically, and the exchange dropped pit trading altogether at the end of February 2008. ICE also almost pulled off a coup to acquire the CBOT until CBOT members voted to merge with the more established CME, but ICE came back from that setback by acquiring the Winnipeg Commodity Exchange.

- The NYSE and other stock exchanges have taken various routes to move into commodities and futures markets; and futures exchanges have returned the favor by moving into the realm of equities markets and the fixed-income arena that has long been the domain of the over-the-counter marketplace.

- Many exchange alliances went international in a fren-
  zied rush to form links with partners in other parts of the
  world. The NYSE's high-profile merger with the Paris-
  based Euronext is only one of many recent agreements by
  exchanges to expand their business to new territories and
  new markets.

- Sovereign states have even gotten a piece of the trading
  action as Middle Eastern countries such as Dubai and
  Qatar, flush with cash from their oil revenues, went on
  shopping sprees to purchase large stakes in the Nasdaq
  Stock Market, London Stock Exchange, and Sweden's
  OMX Market in complex arrangements that open up a
  whole new range of issues related to regulation and secu-
  rity. It remains to be seen how U.S. and other international
  exchanges will be able to compete against such oil-rich
  countries in their efforts to become bigger players on the
  world stage. Joining the exchange fray in recent years has
  been a number of new electronic communication networks
  (ECNs). They have taken a share of trading from traditional exchange centers, helped in part in the United States
  by the March 2007 inauguration of the National Marketing
  System, which mandated that order flow be directed to the
  exchange offering the best price for customers. Among
  these is BATS (an acronym for Better Alternative Trading
  System) Trading Inc. in Kansas City, Mo., far removed
  from the financial centers of New York and Chicago. Major
  brokerage firms and banks such as Merrill Lynch, Morgan
  Stanley, Credit Suisse, and others own stakes in BATS and

other ECNs as they move to minimize trading costs and compete more aggressively for customers.

• New exchange alliances and efficiencies of electronic trading open the financial markets to a broader audience for new contracts based on markets that were not even envisioned just a few years ago—contracts based on carbon emissions and other factors related to global environmental issues like hurricanes, snowfall, and temperatures in major cities; housing futures; new twists for credit derivatives; and a number of other areas as exchanges devise innovative new instruments and ways to manage risk and go head-to-head with the competition provided by over-the-counter arrangements.

These are just some of the developments that are changing the face of the trading industry in the first decade of the 21st century—you almost need a scorecard to keep track of the changes every month. Now both sophisticated traders as well as novices realize that they have to take more interest in looking beyond just one market to the convergence of many related markets, not just geographically but also in product areas, as more attention is focused on risk management on a 24-hour global basis.

It is no longer far-fetched to imagine that some day soon there will be one totally comprehensive electronic global trading network combining major equities and commodity exchanges throughout the world without the turf concerns about where a brick-and-mortar exchange is located. Concepts of "after hours trading," "extended trading," and "open outcry" will undoubtedly become historical footnotes to our lexicon, just as the "buggy whip" and the "horseless carriage" were relegated at the dawn of the 20th century.

Advances in technology and electronic trading will continue the evolution of how trading is conducted and, of course, will influence how firms and individual traders approach a 24-hour marketplace where literally thousands of financial instruments, including esoteric ones not yet conceived, can be traded. Even small institutional trading organizations will need to staff their trading operations around the clock, and many individual traders may suffer from insomnia; they may feel compelled to check their market positions at all hours of the day or night with the concern and worry that there is the potential for some cataclysmic, overnight worldwide meltdown of the financial markets, precipitated by any number of triggering events in today's post 9/11 world.

With advances in the Internet and personal computer capabilities, the speedup in the dissemination of information will continue to push many traders into adopting shorter-term trading strategies as the concept of "buy and hold" as a conservative trading strategy falls by the wayside and is replaced by more aggressive, short-term approaches. After all, an uptrend is an uptrend; a trend reversal is a trend reversal. Patterns will repeat themselves, regardless of the timeframe or label that is put on a market, whether it is pork bellies, the S&P 500 Index, the euro, or Intel. The worldwide intermingling of (and blurring of the lines between) equities and futures will continue to accelerate and create new opportunities and challenges for traders.

EMERGING ECONOMIC FORCES

The trading world, of course, does not exist or function in isolation. It is one facet in an ongoing stream of interconnected events that influences and is influenced by other economic, political, and social factors—from new products and concepts to changes in political structures. Here is a brief recap of a few of the more significant technological, economic, financial, and political forces that have converged to bring about the globalization of the world's financial markets in the first decade of the 21st century:

Advancements in information technologies including computers, satellite, software, and telecommunications. These are focused on the global expansion and commercialization of the Internet and the development of electronic global communications and trading networks. Transactions involving the purchase and sale of financial instruments, tangible property, and the raising of capital will be conducted freely, instantaneously, and competitively on a worldwide level. These developments will render obsolete the concepts of local financial markets and economic nationalism.

• Expansion of global derivatives trading involving interest rate futures, stock indexes, options, and debt-related ETFs. The marriage of derivatives trading with information technologies will continue to meld previously disparate markets, further increasing market interdependencies and bringing about the total internationalization of the financial markets.

• Increased global free trade and competition and the globalization of multinational corporate financing strategies involving capital formation, hedging of foreign exchange and interest rate risk, cross-border listing of shares on multiple exchanges in different countries, corporate consolidations, and cooperative competition through global alliances and mergers and acquisitions (particularly within brokerage, investment banking, and telecommunications, as well as between exchanges) across national boundaries.

- Government deregulation involving the banking, brokerage, energy, telecommunications, and transportation industries. Reductions in marginal tax rates, which stimulate economic activity and global competition; reallocation of capital geographically and from the public to the private sector; increased productivity, lowered costs, and spurred innovation in the development of new technologies.

- Productivity gains brought about by advancements in information technologies positively affecting the cost structure of corporate enterprises and streamlining and shortening supply chains and customer channels.

- Demographic increases in demand for financial assets and broader participation in privatized, tax-deferred profit-sharing and retirement plans by baby boomers.

- Demographic demands resulting from the emergence of a burgeoning middle-class in such countries as China, India, South Korea, and elsewhere for many products and services. As they continue to open up their economic and financial institutions to the broader global economy there will be vast opportunities in regions representing potentially billions of new participants to trade within the global financial markets. The significance of these growing markets can be compared to the economic gains after the fall of the Berlin Wall and the breakup of the former Soviet Union but with much larger potential impact on the global economy and financial markets.

- Emergence of democratically elected governments, increased personal rights, free enterprise, private ownership, the privatization of formerly state-owned enterprises, the encouragement of the spirit of entrepreneurship, and the adoption of market-based economics in developing countries throughout the world, as well as the expansion of free trade as more countries agree to the requirements of, and are welcomed into, the World Trade Organization.

CRISES . . . AND OPPORTUNITIES

All of these factors, as well as others, have ushered in a new era in which there will eventually be just one globally integrated network of financial markets into which all futures, equity, debt, and derivative markets fit as interdependent parts—like pieces in a giant jigsaw puzzle. You already hear or read comments daily about the "global economy" in the financial media or from money managers, corporate executives, or economists. The global voice, data, and video telecommunications will continue to encompass previously independent financial markets, leveling the information playing field by affording various segments of the trading community access to timely information previously only available to sophisticated and institutional traders.

Now, news is beamed around the world instantly by satellite on CNN, CNBC, Fox News, and over the Internet. When there is an unexpected change in a government economic report, a terrorist attack, or if the U.S. Federal Reserve Board or European Central Bank announces a change in interest rates or an Asian country devalues its currency, the proliferation of news agencies makes it possible to know the situation immediately, as it is happening. Within seconds billions of dollars in "hot money" chasing the best returns can be converted and redeployed anywhere around the world electronically at the touch of a mouse button by large international hedge funds and institutional traders without regard to national, political, social, or economic consequences, geographical considerations, or time of day. A well-placed rumor or fictitious press release, perhaps instigated by a new breed of global cyber-saboteur, can now ignite a spark that triggers events globally with instantaneous and potentially devastating financial ramifications, even if the false information is subsequently proven to be unfounded.

There have already been several instances in the recent past of the financial market equivalent of an earthquake of global proportions: the stock market crash of 1987, the Asian and Russian financial market crises in the late 1990s, the market disruption and crash following the terrorist attacks in the United States on September 11, 2001, when the world's futures and equity markets cascaded downward like dominoes falling against each other. More recently, in the summer of 2007 global equity, debt, and forex markets reacted sharply to the worsening crisis that began in the United States involving mortgage debt and credit risk. Fortunately, catastrophic damage to the world's financial markets and economies has been averted so far, but these episodes set the stage for what will undoubtedly dot the world financial landscape in the 21st century, even under the most optimistic global economic scenarios.

As advancements in telecommunications and information technologies accelerate, time-sensitive global market information has become more widely available over the Internet. As electronic day-trading of stocks, futures, ETFs and mutual funds becomes more widespread, such financial earthquakes may make uncharted levels of intraday and interday market volatility commonplace in the 21st century. The possibility of "normal" market selloffs and corrections, which may be very painful and costly to the unwary, has by no means been erased by the new economic paradigm involving the global economy. On the contrary, in the future I surmise that the definition of "normal" may need revision as global crises occur more frequently and with greater impact.

Crisis control by the various sectors of the world's financial markets, including stock and futures exchanges, central banks, clearing organizations, finance ministries, regulatory organizations, and international banking institutions, unfortunately continues to operate on an ad hoc basis. Would the existence of a totally interdependent global communications and trading network, toward which the world's financial markets are steam rolling, mitigate or exacerbate future global financial crises? The answer to this critical question is still an unknown and will only be discovered following a global financial meltdown when the "system" is put to the ultimate test, sort of the way the levees were tested in New Orleans during Hurricane Katrina. If your infrastructure is engineered to withstand a CAT 3 hurricane but you suffer a CAT 5 hit, all bets are off.

I wrote editorials about this impending problem in two articles entitled "Build a global safety net" in February 1990 in the Journal of Commerce and "24-hour Trading: Let's do it right" in April 1990 in Futures magazine. That's nearly two decades ago, yet international organizations are still talking about (but doing very little to actually resolve) these serious issues. This is reminiscent of how the United States has been "talking about" the need for energy independence since the 1973 Arab oil embargo but has done virtually nothing to achieve it. Now that's what I call taking pre-emptive steps to avoid acute oil shortages or a worldwide financial system meltdown that would ripple through the U.S. economy and spread worldwide faster—and with potentially more devastation—than if terrorists were to unleash a dirty bomb in a major U.S. city. Whether it's a bridge collapse in Minnesota, a levee breach in New Orleans, or a near meltdown of the global financial system, why does it have to take a disaster before real preventative action is taken? But, even during such times of crisis, there will always be winners and losers. This is the power of global capitalism at work.

WHO WINS? WHO LOSES?

In this scenario, the distinction between the financial "haves" and "have nots" will be determined by which traders have access to and utilize the most robust analytic tools and information necessary to act decisively and with confidence, particularly at the onset of instability in the financial markets before the situation actually becomes a full-blown crisis. This tug-of-war is especially critical for the tens of millions of baby boomers in the United States, Europe, Asia, and elsewhere who, over the next decade, will desperately need to build and protect their wealth to carry them through their retirement years (potentially lengthened by extended life expectancies due to breakthroughs in medical biotechnology).

Unfortunately, in today's economic climate, with savings accounts and money market funds and other investments offering minimal returns, with equities at constant risk of sharp setbacks, and with the decline in housing values cutting into their net worth, these baby boomers don't have many places to turn for growth potential and liquidity unless they become more involved as traders in the global futures, forex, and equity markets. These realizations are what prompted me in the mid-1980s to focus my attention on the broader framework of intermarket analysis and global markets to forecast short-term trends and prices based upon the pattern recognition capabilities that can be realized through the application of intermarket data to a form of artificial intelligence known as neural networks.

This approach addresses four important questions that I believe every trader must grapple with each day:

- Which direction is the market heading?

- When will the current trend begin to lose strength, make a top or bottom, and begin to reverse direction?

- How strong will the next move be?

- What will tomorrow's trading range be?

This book takes you through the steps of intermarket analysis to show you how it can provide a more comprehensive data set that can be analyzed in order for you to gain an early edge in forecasting market trends that can dramatically improve your trading performance.

Chapter 2

TECHNICAL ANALYSIS FOR TODAY'S MARKETS

Historically, the methods that have been used by traders to analyze financial markets in an effort to identify and forecast the direction of price trends have been divided into two distinct approaches: fundamental analysis and technical analysis.

Fundamental analysis is used by traders to make trading decisions by forecasting future prices and the trend direction on the basis of underlying economic factors affecting a particular financial market. For example, traders may decide to buy U.S. Treasury notes because they anticipate their prices will increase following the onset of a global crisis when traders exhibit a flight to quality. This is exactly what happened in 2007 as concerns over credit risk in the United States spread worldwide. In another scenario, traders may buy corn because they expect crop losses due to expected drought conditions or higher demand due to an increase in ethanol production. They may buy shares of Intel because they expect this stock to beat the Street's quarterly earnings estimates or Google because of the shift among advertisers to the Internet from more traditional media such as newspapers and magazines.

Every market is affected by a multitude of fundamental factors. The difficulty is getting reliable information before the rest of the marketplace knows it, sorting out what really will drive prices, and anticipating correctly how other traders will react to this fundamental information, whether it's a weather forecast or statistics in a government economic report. In other words, it can be a significant challenge to arrive at a sound and timely trading decision by considering all of the fundamental influences on a given market at a specific point in time.

FOCUSING ON ONE FACTOR

The premise behind technical analysis, which is contrary to that of fundamental analysis, is that all of the internal and external factors that are thought to affect a market at any given point in time are already built into that market's price, even if these factors are based on fundamentals or mass-psychology. This price-discovery mechanism is one of the key underlying premises of technical analysis of the financial markets. In other words, a market's current price is thought to reflect the rational collective judgment of all market participants, each with their own information on that market and their own perception of what they anticipate the market trend direction is likely to be in the immediate or near future.

If the assumption that the current price fully discounts all of the available information about that market and the influences or forces affecting it is correct, then traders who rely on technical analysis would have no reason to delve into any of the underlying economic factors thought to influence the market.

Instead, technically-oriented traders concentrate on using various technical studies, indicators, and market-forecasting theories to analyze market behavior, without digging deeper in the economic factors such as supply and demand statistics, which are the bread and butter of fundamental analysis. By examining historical market data such as price, volume, and open interest on any given market, technical analysts attempt to discern repetitive patterns in the data that can be used to help identify the current market trend, forecast or infer the market's future trend direction and prices, and provide price targets for entry and exit points.

WHAT'S THE MARKET TREND?

Although fundamental analysis and technical analysis each have their own underlying philosophical foundation and specific analytic methodologies that look at the markets from two different viewpoints, both methods of analysis have essentially the same goal; namely determining the future trend direction of the various financial markets. It doesn't matter whether the market is an individual stock, stock index, interest rate, currency or commodity future, the key questions in both types of analysis are:

- What is the current trend direction?

- How strong is the current trend?

- How long is the current trend likely to continue?

- When will the trend change direction?

By asking these questions and analyzing either fundamental or technical data, traders are able to make trading decisions based on their conclusions about market direction with the intent to realize a profit if their market forecasts and timing prove to be correct.

Adherents of both technical and fundamental analysis each believe that their type of analysis will lead to superior trading performance. In short, you have one common goal that is looked at from two different perspectives. The question of which is the more effective approach has been a controversial subject over the years, with countervailing arguments that the conduct of technical and fundamental analysis is an effort in futility.

In an article in Barron's in March 1989 entitled, "It's time to combine fundamental and technical analysis for a total game plan" and two years later in September 1991 in an editorial entitled "It's time to rethink the role of technical analysis" in the Market Technicians Association newsletter, I have spoken out on this controversial subject, proposing that a comprehensive approach is necessary for success.

I believe that making implicit or explicit short-term trend forecasts based upon some form of pattern recognition on past data (whether it's technical, fundamental, and/or intermarket data) improves the caliber of the decision-making process, which will lead to more profitable trading. That holds true whether the forecast is made with subjective chart or data analysis or more rigorous quantitative analysis such as the work that I have done with neural networks applied to intermarket data. However, even if a trader were fortunate enough to produce a perfectly accurate forecast of the market direction, he or she would still have one final challenge to surmount—the matter of "market timing."

PLAY THE MARKETS OR TIME THE MARKETS?

Once traders analyze a specific market and form an opinion about the likely trend direction of that market, they must still decide when to get in or out of a position and at what price. As in many other walks of life, timing is everything. In today's global financial markets, even if you were able to forecast the trend direction 100% correctly, you could still end up losing money if your timing is off by even one day.

Market timing is especially challenging for futures and forex traders because of the risk involved due to their low capital requirements and high degree of leverage. Timing has also become an issue in the equities markets as the new breed of electronic day-traders spawned in the last decade move into and out of fast-moving individual stocks and ETFs, with the same speed that futures traders buy and sell contracts on the Japanese yen or the S&P 500 Index. More equity traders now have to concern themselves with market timing than ever before.

As a trader, nothing is more frustrating than anticipating the trend direction correctly, getting into a position a little too soon, having the market go against you, getting stopped out and then watching the market turn around and move in the direction that you expected. When this scenario occurs, you either sit on the sidelines after having taken a loss or try to chase after the market. Both alternatives are very frustrating.

So, it is not just identifying the trend direction that is important. You also need to be able to anticipate when the market is poised to make a top or a bottom and change direction. When you 1) have a reasonably accurate forecast of the expected trend direction, 2) can identify impending turning points, and 3) have a good idea of the next day's price range to help you determine entry and exit prices and set stops, you really have done your analysis. Now it's just a matter of having the self-discipline and confidence to "pull the trigger." This is where the psychology of trading comes into play.

STRATEGIES THAT ANTICIPATE, NOT REACT

Because the main objective of technical analysis is trend identification and forecasting, it would stand to reason that this goal could best be achieved by developing trading strategies that can somehow anticipate changes in trend direction, rather than ones that lag the market.

Many single-market technical analysis indicators such as support and resistance lines, moving averages, and chart pattern formations are popular lagging indicators that look internally at an individual market's past price history and attempt to extrapolate from that data reoccurring price patterns that might prove useful for forecasting. This type of analysis really boils down to looking at what the market has already done and trying to guess where it is going next.

Despite frustration and disappointment with their trading results, many traders still use such lagging indicators, which were first popularized before personal computers came on the scene 30 years ago. Instead, I have advocated that traders, to be successful, need analysis tools that act as leading indicators; so, traders can anticipate price action and identify whether or not the current trend is likely to continue or is on the verge of changing direction.

TYPICAL ROUTE TO TECHNICAL ANALYSIS

Novice traders seem to follow a familiar learning path as they get involved in the financial markets for the first time. First, they learn the ABCs of technical analysis by reading a few introductory books or magazine articles, by watching educational videos, attending webinars, or going to conferences and seminars. These traders learn about price formations and chart patterns such as head-and-shoulders, flags, islands, pennants, triangles, support and resistance trend lines, gap patterns, and price channels. They may also learn how to apply other trend-following, lagging indicators, such as moving averages, which are still very popular despite their limitations.

Pick up a current issue of any popular financial magazine, and you will find articles on technical analysis with current charts and graphs and hypothetical profitability reports that are virtually identical in content to articles that were published in the financial press in the 1970s, 1980s, and 1990s on the exact same subject. The only difference is the dates on the charts. But the content and focus of the articles have not changed an iota. Although such updated articles are undoubtedly enlightening to newcomers to trading who are just beginning to learn about technical analysis and the financial markets, such articles prove that the revolving door of traders is due in part to their reliance on totally outdated and inadequate approaches that have not kept pace at all with the interconnectedness of today's global financial markets.

> The revolving door of traders is due in part to their reliance on totally outdated and inadequate approaches that have not kept pace at all with the interconnectedness of today's global financial markets.

If you are an experienced trader, maybe you can recall how excited you were when you first learned about "exponential" moving averages or "stochastics" and, more important, understood how they are used to analyze market trends. I cannot even begin to count how many dozens of articles and books on technical analysis I have read over the last 35 years discussing various types of moving averages and comparing their effectiveness at reducing the lag.

This subject was covered in detail in Perry Kaufman's *Commodity Trading Systems and Methods* originally published in 1978 and in Charles Patel's *Technical Trading Systems for Commodities and Stocks* published in 1980—to name just two classics in my personal library. I even have an article in my research files on curvilinear regression analysis for forecasting the live cattle market, published in Commodities magazine in 1974. Surely there's got to be something more robust than hashed-over technical analysis approaches that predate personal computers. Just think where we would be today in the field of medicine if the approaches still practiced predated the founding of Genentech. We'd probably have a futures market for leeches and medical webinars on bloodletting.

Today, after getting their appetites whetted by reading about technical analysis, traders often pursue their newfound interest by purchasing mass-marketed technical analysis software programs, which automate and perform the calculations of various single-market, lagging indicators. After developing and testing their trading strategies built around some of these concepts, these traders delude themselves into thinking that they are on the verge of getting rich quick and will soon be able to quit their day jobs to become full-time traders. Nothing could be further from the truth.

LEARNING PAINFUL LESSONS

Although many of today's newcomers to trading have witnessed 250-300 point down days in the Dow Jones Industrial Average recently, they have little, if any, personal knowledge of some of the stock market routs or crashes of the past, when the decline on a percentage basis was much greater than these recent setbacks. They may not have experienced the emotional turmoil immediately following the September 11, 2001 terrorist attack, or the pain following the 1987 crash, not to mention the torturous decline of 1974 when the Dow dropped nearly 50% from its previous high.

I experienced my first painful and unforgettable lesson about the psychological struggle between greed and fear in 1974 when fear ultimately demonstrated its more powerful grip on the human psyche. One of my defensive utility stocks, ConEd, which I held onto thinking it would weather the storm because of its hefty dividend, actually did the unthinkable: It suspended its quarterly dividend, which it had paid continuously since the late 1800s including during the Great

Depression that followed the 1929 stock market crash. Within hours, my $20.00 stock plunged to $6.00 on the bad news—and this was no two-bit penny-stock. It was Consolidated Edison! Today, such a plunge would take seconds to occur.

Bull markets that chug upward for weeks or months with little or no retracement cause novice traders to overestimate their trading skills. Protracted bull markets make nearly everyone think of themselves as a Wall Street trading guru. This is a dangerous phenomenon. Even my 85-year-old mother-in-law, Kitty Greenspan (no relation to Alan), who I love dearly, got caught up in this process during the late 1990s tech bubble and again in 2007 as the Dow continued to break new record highs and then hit a rough patch. Her emotions act as a barometer of how the market is doing each day, as up days are followed by down days, and volatility increases with each new broken record. Greed seduces traders into developing unrealistically high expectations of annual market returns and an underestimation of the risks inherent in trading. Under such circumstances, traders first develop an inflated, false sense of self-confidence in which they come to expect quick profits with every trade and with little risk. This is invariably then followed by the shock of losing money that, in many cases, they were not emotionally prepared to lose.

Too often, traders assume that a heavily advertised or inexpensive trading tool must be the one to use—after all, so many other traders have already bought it. Unfortunately, technical analysis tools are not like inexpensive DVD players, where the most popular one is perhaps the best.

FOLLOWING THE HERD

At the same time, traders are increasingly getting market information—as well as misinformation and even "disinformation"—from a handful of common sources, such as financial television networks, popular websites, chat forums, and free webinars. Too often, alluring infomercials on forex trading or gold bullion investments fuel the fire by suggesting that wealth can be acquired quickly without much work. This makes today's generation of traders even more prone to herd behavior and susceptible to get-rich-quick schemes.

This herd instinct mentality results in a psychological phenomenon sometimes referred to as "thought contagion," which contributes in no small part to loss statistics among traders. In the case of futures traders, for instance, it is reported that upwards of 95% of them lose their money after a short stint at trading. If the airline industry had a comparable fatality record, no one in their right mind would set foot on a commercial plane, and Amtrak would be hailed as the safest, most convenient way to travel cross country.

Think about it rationally for a minute. If a high percentage of individual traders rely upon the same sort of single-market analysis tools and information sources that lag behind the markets and ignore global market dynamics, and if an overwhelming percentage of those traders end up losing their trading capital, then doesn't it stand to reason that, if you decide to follow the herd, you will end up exactly like them? We see this same behavior in teenagers who get caught up with illegal drugs and other self-destructive behaviors. They rationalize their actions by thinking to themselves, "I'm different; it won't happen to me." Yet, when it comes to trading, this same type of peer group influence that comes from following the masses doesn't trigger any alarms.

If the masses of traders are all looking at the markets from the same narrow, market-by-market perspective, and if they lose their money while doing so, you should expect similar results if you perform the same kinds of analysis that they do. Common sense would tell you that you'll lose your money, too. It doesn't take a rocket scientist to figure this equation out, yet unfortunately too many newcomers to the markets start off on the wrong foot, end up losing their trading capital, and are forced to quit trading not long after they began.

TAKING OFF TECHNICAL ANALYSIS BLINDERS

Technical analysis is still much too limited in scope, looking internally at one market at a time with little regard for the external intermarket factors that also influence that market. Additionally, relatively little progress has been made at objectively (quantitatively rather than subjectively) identifying repetitive price patterns necessary to perform effective market forecasting. Instead of forecasting future trends in a way that captures the character and nature of today's globally interdependent financial markets, traditional single-market technical analysis is still performed retrospectively by extrapolating past price data on a single market into the future, just as it had been practiced in the years before the emergence of the globalization of the financial markets, and, as we've discussed, even before there were personal computers.

An overwhelming percentage of traders, particularly those new to the equity, futures, and forex markets in the last few years and those with small amounts of trading capital, are still either unfamiliar with, close-minded to, or just plain intimidated by intermarket analysis for whatever reason. They continue to wear restrictive technical analysis blinders; content to focus their attention on only one futures market, forex pair, or individual stock at a time, as if that market was trading in complete isolation. The result is a misperception of what is really happening—and, more important, what is about to happen—in that market.

No wonder so many traders act like spooked horses as soon as the markets get a little choppy or have a sudden trend reversal. These traders hear and read everyday about the global economy and how markets throughout the world are interconnected and linked to one another . . . but they do not really know how to analyze the vast amount of market data this is readily available. So they continue to rely upon outdated single-market, lagging indicators and cross their fingers and hope that a global financial meltdown doesn't catch them off guard when they forgot to put a trailing stop on their positions—or, worse yet, during another trading time zone when they are asleep.

If this is how you approach your trading, it means that you are making your trading decisions without knowing relevant factors, which affect the markets you trade. This is a disaster waiting to happen. If you have a small account to work with, your situation is even more precarious because every trade must count. There is little room for error. If you are in this situation, as far as I am concerned, you should stop trading immediately and get your act together before getting back into the markets. If you are not willing to learn about the markets, study the basic mechanics of trading, and focus your attention on the global interconnectedness of today's markets, then you shouldn't be trading. There is no shortcut. You've got to be willing to put the effort into studying and learning about the markets and then get the right analytic tools— before you put any money at risk. This is where websites such as www. TraderPlanet.com can really help you shorten the learning curve.

It is a fallacy to think that when you first start trading you can get by using cheap, commonly used, single-market analysis tools to build up your trading account until you can "afford" to get the right tools. In theory, this approach sounds plausible; in reality, you're more likely to lose all of your money. You will struggle to break even, at best, if not be driven out of the markets. You cannot put the cart before the horse.

Get the right tools from the get-go and do your homework, or don't even bother trading until you do.

Here's a simple analogy: If your spouse develops a life-threatening heart condition, you wouldn't choose a cardiologist based on how inexpensive his fees are with the intention that after her condition improves a little, you'll switch to a better doctor. That would be ridiculous. If you want the treatment to be successful, you would consult with the best doctor you can find from the beginning.

Similarly, to get the best diagnosis and prognosis of market behavior, you need to have the best analytic tools that are available—and even then, you need to work hard at being a successful trader. Nothing good comes easy. Trading is like playing golf. To be successful, you need to do your homework, study the markets, learn about the mechanics of trading, develop strategies that suit your own trading style and risk propensity, and test the waters with limited risk before you jump in head first. As golf legend Gary Player has said "the harder you practice, the luckier you get." Remember, the markets will always be there, so there is no rush to trade until you are confident that you know what you are doing.

> If your trading strategies do not factor in the linkages between related markets, then you are blind to the market synergy that drives today's globally interconnected markets.

Although a market-by-market analysis of each individual market by itself is still necessary, it is no longer sufficient because it fails to take into consideration present-day circumstances involving the global nature of today's markets. If your trading strategies do not factor in the linkages between related markets, then you are blind to the market synergy that drives today's globally interconnected markets.

MAINTAINING A BROAD FOCUS

As market globalization becomes even more pervasive and fast-paced in the coming years, those traders who limit their focus to a single market's past prices or who still rely only on subjective chart pattern analysis or linear forecasting methods (such as correlation analysis between two markets) will pay the price as they watch their trading accounts dwindle. On the other hand, astute traders will be able to take advantage of unprecedented opportunities to amass substantial wealth through their involvement in the global financial markets.

Single-market methods of analysis, particularly trend-following, lagging approaches, worked reasonably well over the last few decades when the markets were less volatile and tended to trade independently of one another. However, such approaches needed to be replaced long ago by more robust analytic tools with forecasting capabilities that address the interconnected context of trading in today's global financial markets. We'll get to that, but first we need to lay the groundwork with some basic technical analysis concepts so that you can put all of this into an historical context.

Chapter 3

CHART PATTERNS:
BUILDING BLOCKS OF TECHNICAL ANALYSIS

One of the underlying purposes of technical analysis is to identify when a market is trending and when it is not. Therefore, it is important for a new trader to start his study of technical analysis with the definition of a trend before proceeding to learn how to forecast the trend of a market. The simplest definition of a trend is a series of higher highs and higher lows (uptrend) or a series of lower highs and lower lows (downtrend).

If that makes it sound like it should be easy to determine when a market is trending up or down versus when it is in a trading range, keep in mind that markets tend to spend much of their time chopping back and forth within ranges and tend to twist and turn to keep as few traders as possible from riding the trend successfully, even when they have identified a trend—it's a lot like trying to stay on a bucking bronco in a rodeo.

Let's start our discussion with some conclusions on which technical analysts can agree, no matter what approach they each use to identify trends and make their trading decisions:

    1. Everything that is known about a market is reflected in

one thing, the current price. That makes price the center-piece of technical analysis, for better or for worse. We'll talk later about how to find price data that can be more useful in trading than just single-market prices from the past.

2. You cannot look at one price in isolation. If you were told that the price of Market XYZ is 5, is that high or low? Does it indicate the true value of that market? Relative to what? Other prices of the past? Other related markets? You have to put the current price in perspective with prices that occurred previously and with prices of other markets that might be sub-stitutes for, or in competition with, your target market.

3. Charts are the best way to view price action over time, whatever time frame you want to consider. Prices leave behind telltale tracks, and the picture of those tracks on a chart is like a roadmap of price action. Just like a ship captain trying to navigate unknown seas or travelers try-ing to find their way through territory new to them, traders need some kind of navigational map to guide them through their decision-making process. Even those traders who only believe in fundamentals will have to admit they need to have some way to put current prices into historical context.

4. A chart depicts visually what the masses of traders are thinking emotionally in the ongoing struggle between fear and greed. Price action on the chart may not correlate with fundamental data, and price reactions to fundamental information may not always seem to make sense. But, price reflects the collective opinions of the masses, and that's what counts. It is not a force you want to fight if you want to stay in the game as a trader.

CHARTING THE ACTION

Once you accept the above premises, you can use several different types of charts to track price history and thereby gain insight into market action and trend direction.

LINE CHARTS

These charts are based on only one price for a given period, typically the closing price. Often, traders will want to know more than that, but for mutual funds or other markets that feature only one price per day (or any other time period you designate), these charts may be sufficient for viewing the overall trend of a market. Moving averages and other indicators are also depicted as line charts. (See Figure 3.1)

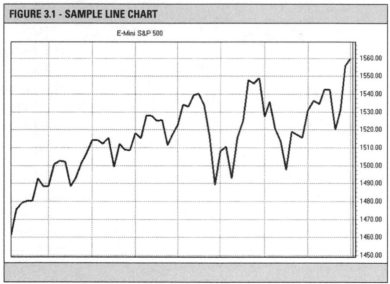

FIGURE 3.1 - SAMPLE LINE CHART

E-Mini S&P 500

VANTAGEPOINT INTERMARKET ANALYSIS SOFTWARE

BAR CHARTS

It is often helpful to know several other pieces of information about a market in addition to just the closing price for a given period. These items include the opening price and the high and low prices for a period, which can all be represented on the bar chart. The open is the small horizontal "tick" mark to the left of the vertical bar; the close is the small horizontal "tick" mark to the right of the vertical bar. These prices tell analysts how far traders were willing to push prices during the period and where the closing price wound up relative to the open, high and low during the period or compared to highs and lows from previous periods. (See Figure 3.2)

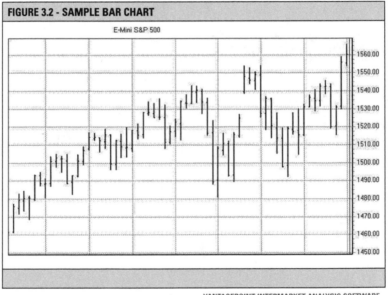

FIGURE 3.2 - SAMPLE BAR CHART

E-Mini S&P 500

VANTAGEPOINT INTERMARKET ANALYSIS SOFTWARE

CANDLESTICK CHARTS

These charts have the same basic information as the bar chart—open, high, low, close. However, candlestick charts present prices with a different twist so the price action during a given period is shown more visually to enhance analysis at a glance. Although these charts have been used in Japan for centuries, they did not really get much notice from Western traders until the late 1980s.

With these charts, the open and close are significant, and the difference between these two prices comprise the "body" of the candle. If the closing price is higher than the opening price, a candle is typically shown as a white or clear color, indicating that price movement during the period was higher or stronger; if the closing price is lower than the opening price, a candle is typically shown as black or solid, indicating that price movement during the period was lower or weaker.

Price action that occurs outside the body's range becomes the period's "tails," "wicks," or "shadows." Although most candle analysis concentrates on the body, because it represents trader thinking during the

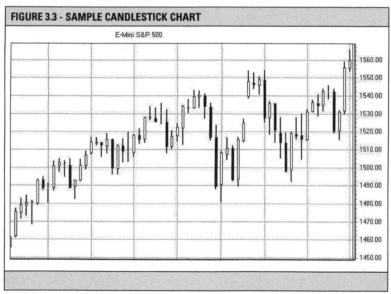

FIGURE 3.3 - SAMPLE CANDLESTICK CHART

E-Mini S&P 500

VANTAGEPOINT INTERMARKET ANALYSIS SOFTWARE

main trading session, tails also provide useful information. For example, if there is a long tail above the body, it means selling had to come into the marketplace to push prices down from the high of the day to the close or open (depending on the type of candle), a potential sign that selling pressure could be strong enough to force prices lower.

Although an individual candle itself can provide important clues about market strength or weakness, much of the "light" that the candle provides depends on its location within a series of other candles and is valuable for longer-term analysis of a series of candles. (See Figure 3.3)

DIFFERENT LOOKS, SAME ANALYSIS

Whatever type of chart you decide to use—there is no right or wrong choice—your first step in technical analysis should be to detect the trend of the market.

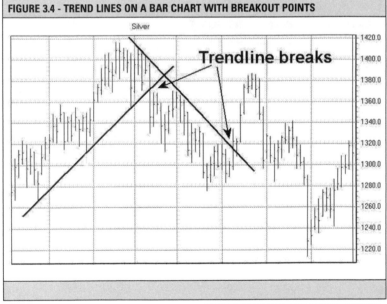

FIGURE 3.4 - TREND LINES ON A BAR CHART WITH BREAKOUT POINTS

VANTAGEPOINT INTERMARKET ANALYSIS SOFTWARE

"The importance of trading in the direction of the major trend cannot be overstated," says noted technical analyst John J. Murphy in his classic book, *Technical Analysis of the Futures Markets*. "The danger in placing too much importance on oscillators, by themselves, is the temptation to use divergence as an excuse to initiate trades contrary to the general trend. This action generally proves a costly and painful exercise. The oscillator, as useful as it is, is just one tool among many others and must always be used as an aid, not a substitute, for basic trend analysis."

A trend in motion tends to stay in motion—until it doesn't. Trends always end at some point, marked by the penetration of the trend line. (See Figure 3.4)

It often is helpful to draw a line parallel to the main trend line to form a trading channel, giving the trend boundaries within which prices fluc-

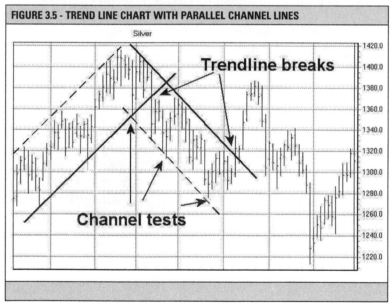

FIGURE 3.5 - TREND LINE CHART WITH PARALLEL CHANNEL LINES

VANTAGEPOINT INTERMARKET ANALYSIS SOFTWARE

tuate. Channels clarify the trend and can help traders spot breakouts in either direction. (See Figure 3.5)

Drawing trend lines is not an exact science. A glance at any chart usually reveals a general trend or lack of trend to even the most novice trader, but refining that trend into an actual trading plan can be more of an art, depending on what the beholder "sees." And one beholder may not see precisely what another beholder does, depending on the time frame of the chart and what the beholder is trying to determine.

In the descriptions of any chart pattern, keep in mind that traders are dealing with probabilities or tendencies based on what has happened when the market has exhibited similar patterns in the past. There is no guarantee that a chart pattern, no matter how clear or strong it may appear to be, will follow through like the textbook suggests it should.

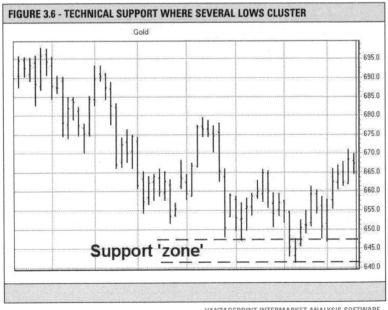

FIGURE 3.6 - TECHNICAL SUPPORT WHERE SEVERAL LOWS CLUSTER

Gold

Support 'zone'

695.0
690.0
685.0
680.0
675.0
670.0
665.0
660.0
655.0
650.0
645.0
640.0

VANTAGEPOINT INTERMARKET ANALYSIS SOFTWARE

CHART PATTERNS

Before looking at some of the major chart patterns, several concepts need to be introduced because they are an integral part of many chart patterns. They provide some predictive or measurement capabilities that can guide a trader who relies on chart patterns to make trading decisions.

SUPPORT AND RESISTANCE

Technical analysis begins with the trend line, and we have already alluded to the fact that the trend line is also the first point of support and resistance. A trend line along the lows in an uptrend denotes support, and a trend line along the highs in a downtrend shows the line of resistance, as illustrated in Figure 3.4. They are key barriers for prices to cross if the market is to change trend direction.

Trend lines aren't the only source of support and resistance. Check out a chart to see at what price levels the highs, lows, and closes seem to be touching the most. Many times several highs or lows will be concentrated in a small price area but not at one specific price. That provides a support or resistance "zone" that should be rather narrow to be effective. (See Figure 3.6)

Major price bottoms and tops from the past are also major support and resistance levels. Unfilled price gaps on charts also qualify as support and resistance levels. Similarly, moving averages, especially longer-term ones, can also provide support or resistance.

Support and resistance levels also can be determined by "psychological" price levels—usually significant round numbers such as $80 a barrel for crude oil, $800 an ounce for gold, or 60 cents a pound for cotton. These levels mark clear steps where the market often pauses to reassess the situation.

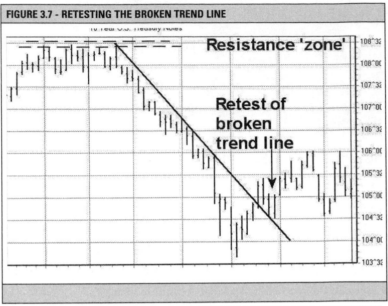

FIGURE 3.7 - RETESTING THE BROKEN TREND LINE

Resistance 'zone'

Retest of broken trend line

VANTAGEPOINT INTERMARKET ANALYSIS SOFTWARE

Another common pattern you will see on a price chart occurs when a key support level or zone is penetrated by a price move to the downside. Prices are likely to move back up to that level or zone again to test whether that breakdown is for real, and what was once support then becomes key resistance. Likewise, a key resistance level or zone that is penetrated on the upside is likely to be retested as prices drift back down, and it then often becomes a key support level or zone. (See Figure 3.7)

Retracements

"Retracements" can also be a source of support or resistance. After a market runs up or down, prices tend to make moves that are counter to the existing price trend as the market gets "overbought" or "oversold." These moves are also called "corrections."

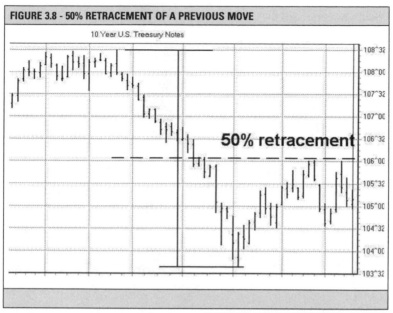

FIGURE 3.8 - 50% RETRACEMENT OF A PREVIOUS MOVE

10 Year U.S. Treasury Notes

50% retracement

VANTAGEPOINT INTERMARKET ANALYSIS SOFTWARE

When a market breaks through a trend line, traders try to assess how far the correction might extend. Based on studies of past price history, a popular retracement target is 50% of the previous trend. For example, in an uptrend if a market rises from 50 to 100 and starts a correction, traders might look for a 50% retracement or a move from 100 back to 75. They would anticipate prices might bounce back up off that level and resume the uptrend. If the correction retracement is less than 50%, that suggests a stronger market; if the retracement is more than 50%, it indicates a weaker market.

The 50% mark isn't the only popular retracement level. Some analysts use the 33% and 67% levels as support or resistance. Fibonacci advocates use ratios of 0.382% and 0.618% of a prior move as key support and resistance targets and make their trading decisions on the basis of how the market reacts when it approaches those levels. (See Figure 3.8)

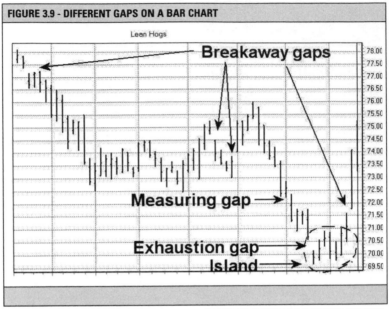

FIGURE 3.9 - DIFFERENT GAPS ON A BAR CHART

VANTAGEPOINT INTERMARKET ANALYSIS SOFTWARE

Gaps

Gaps are areas on a price chart where no trading occurs. For example, the last bar's low is higher than the previous bar's high for a gap-higher move. Gaps tend to occur after periods when the market has been closed and overnight or weekend news gives traders a different view on value. With electronic trading 24 hours a day, gaps are less likely to appear as the market moves more fluidly from one price to the next.

Although not all price gaps are significant, they typically suggest a strong opinion shift about a market, and the gap then serves as an important support or resistance level on the chart. How you read the message of the gap usually depends on where it occurs on the chart. (See Figure 3.9)

Breakaway gaps occur at the beginning of a move as prices reject the previous trend and suddenly reverse course, or they may be found at the breakout point of a chart formation such as a trend line or a triangle. The breakaway may be the result of traders learning new information or because buy/sell demand has built up during the time while the market was closed.

Measuring gaps are a little trickier to label as they often cannot be identified until after the fact. As the market moves up or down, it may suddenly leave a gap higher or lower because of some new development that becomes known as the market continues its existing trend. Some analysts view the gap as the halfway point between the previous high or low and an ultimate price objective. If the gap's projection coincides with a well-defined support or resistance area such as a previous high or low, it gives traders confidence that the gap's price target might be reached.

Measuring gaps occur roughly midway through an extended move. In Figure 3.9, after prices fell more than $3, the market gapped down on the open from the previous close, enabling analysts to set a downside target another $3 lower.

Exhaustion gaps appear at the end of an extended move and reflect a last burst of buying in an uptrend or selling in a downtrend. After this buying or selling frenzy, no new buyers or sellers are left to maintain the trend, as the power that has been driving the trend is exhausted. The change in the trend may be abrupt and cause a dramatic move in the opposite direction as the late buyers or sellers scramble to unload their losing positions.

Island tops and bottoms combine an exhaustion gap and a breakaway gap and reflect the complete change in market sentiment that sometimes takes place as new conditions become known to traders.

CONTINUATION PATTERNS

As long as prices continue to respect a trend line, then that line is probably the most important continuation pattern you can see on a chart. But a few other chart formations offer clues as to whether a price move is likely to continue.

Bullish Flags

After a strong uptrend, a market tends to need a little time to digest the results before deciding what to do next. A pause or sideways to lower prices for a few periods acts as a small countertrend to the main trend. Then the market resumes a strong price uptrend. The surge off a bottom may look like a flagpole and can be used to measure the extent of a further up-move once prices break out above the flag. (See Figure 3.10)

Bearish Flags

Bearish flag patterns act like bullish flags but in the opposite direction during a strong price downtrend. Prices pause or move sideways to higher for a few periods, then resume the ongoing downtrend. The congestion area gives the market time to consolidate and re-evaluate its situation before resuming its downward trek. (See Figure 3.10)

Symmetrical Triangles and Pennants

Triangle-shaped patterns act much like the bullish and bearish flags except that the price action tends to unfold in a pattern that looks more like a coil as the highs and lows result in smaller and smaller price ranges as they move to the apex of the triangle. The breakout from the

FIGURE 3.10 - BULL AND BEAR FLAGS ON A BAR CHART

Corn

NOTE THAT THE BREAKOUTS ON BOTH FLAGS MARKED ON THIS CHART OCCURRED WITH GAPS.

VANTAGEPOINT INTERMARKET ANALYSIS SOFTWARE

FIGURE 3.11 - PENNANTS ON A BAR CHART

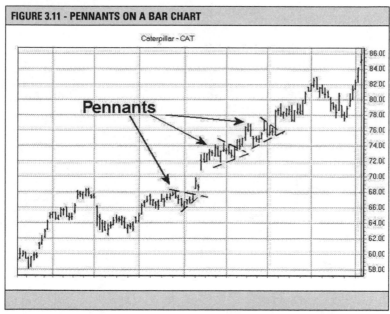

Caterpillar - CAT

VANTAGEPOINT INTERMARKET ANALYSIS SOFTWARE

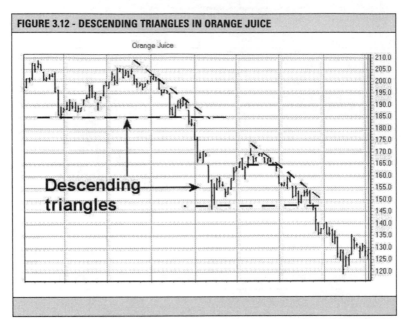

FIGURE 3.12 - DESCENDING TRIANGLES IN ORANGE JUICE

Orange Juice

Descending triangles

VANTAGEPOINT INTERMARKET ANALYSIS SOFTWARE

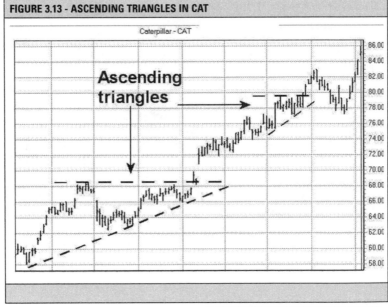

FIGURE 3.13 - ASCENDING TRIANGLES IN CAT

Caterpillar - CAT

Ascending triangles

VANTAGEPOINT INTERMARKET ANALYSIS SOFTWARE

triangle pattern tends to be in the same direction as the dominant price trend that moved into the triangle. (See Figure 3.11)

Descending Triangle

During a downtrend, the market finds buying support at about the same general level for a number of different periods, while the highs drop progressively lower. After the price range narrows into the apex of the triangle, the market breaks below the horizontal price level that had acted as support as traders seem to give up their effort to hold prices at or above that level. The breakout to the downside suggests the downtrend will continue. (See Figure 3.12)

Ascending Triangle

Turn the description of the descending triangle upside down and you have the ascending triangle. Sellers are able to hold prices below a certain level to form the horizontal top of the triangle, while buyers keep pushing the lows of the price range higher. Eventually, the breakout above the horizontal line suggests the bullish forces have won by breaking through resistance, and the uptrend is likely to continue. (See Figure 3.13)

REVERSAL PATTERNS

Like their name implies, these patterns suggest that one trend is ending and the market is ready to begin another trend in the opposite direction or, perhaps more likely, move sideways for a while. As with continuation patterns, a trend line is the basic reference point to watch. If prices break through a trend line

Figure 3.13 may look familiar as it is a repeat of Figure 3.11. But where one trader sees pennants, another may see ascending triangles, illustrating how chart patterns are often in the eye of the beholder.

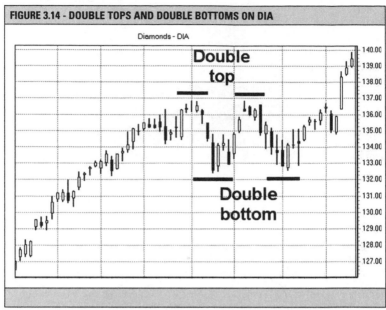

FIGURE 3.14 - DOUBLE TOPS AND DOUBLE BOTTOMS ON DIA

Diamonds - DIA

VANTAGEPOINT INTERMARKET ANALYSIS SOFTWARE

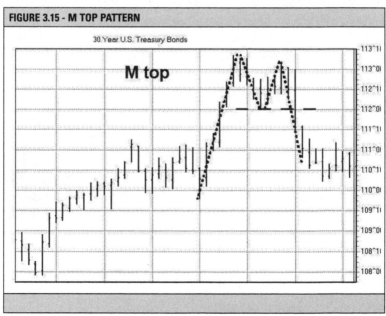

FIGURE 3.15 - M TOP PATTERN

30 Year U.S. Treasury Bonds

VANTAGEPOINT INTERMARKET ANALYSIS SOFTWARE

and then follow through in the same direction in the next period, this is the best evidence of a trend reversal. Keep in mind that all chart patterns apply to all trading time frames—daily, weekly, monthly, yearly, hourly, or even minute-by-minute bar charts.

Double Tops

Prices reach a new high, back off from that high, re-test the high, and back off again. The highs may stand out like radio towers above the rest of the price action. The longer the time between these two peaks, the more powerful the chart pattern is likely to be. These highs represent the extent to which traders are willing to push prices, but they will go no further. The highs can provide a formidable line of horizontal resistance on any attempts to rise above them in the near future. (See Figure 3.14)

Double Bottoms

This pattern is similar to the double-top reversal but naturally is the mirror image on a bottom—the market makes a low, rallies to an interim high, sags back to the previous low, and then rallies. Just like the double top forms strong resistance, the double bottom provides strong support, and prices tend to bounce back up unless the downward trend has some significant selling pressure behind it.

"M" Tops

These patterns are similar to the double top and are also known as 1-2-3 swing tops. In the M pattern, the second high is usually a little lower than the first high, indicating that the market is not quite as strong as it was on the first runup to a high. The highs become a barrier that stops further upward price movement. When prices drop below the interim low between the two highs, the top is confirmed, which is an indication that the market may be reversing into a downtrend. (See Figure 3.15)

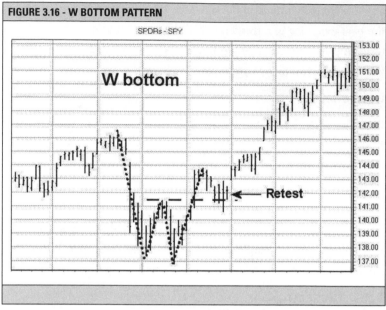

FIGURE 3.16 - W BOTTOM PATTERN

SPDRs - SPY

W bottom

Retest

VANTAGEPOINT INTERMARKET ANALYSIS SOFTWARE

"W" Bottoms

Conversely, in the W bottom or 1-2-3 swing bottom, the second low may be in the same vicinity as the first low of a double bottom or may be a little higher than the first low. When the market rallies off the second low and exceeds the interim high between the two lows, the bottom is confirmed, the pattern is complete, and the market indicates it may be reversing into an uptrend. (See Figure 3.16)

Note that in either the M top or W bottom pattern, the market often comes back to test the breakout point to make sure it is for real. Rather than try to catch the first breakout, a patient trader is often better off waiting for this kickback price action to place an order and avoiding the choppy movement that sometimes accompanies a breakout.

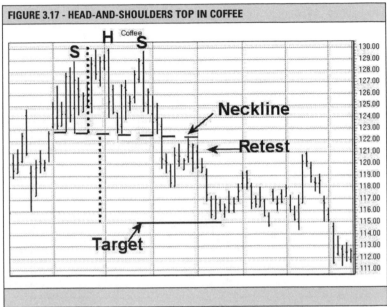

FIGURE 3.17 - HEAD-AND-SHOULDERS TOP IN COFFEE

VANTAGEPOINT INTERMARKET ANALYSIS SOFTWARE

Head-and-shoulders Top

This pattern with the catchy name is really just an extended M top. The market rallies to a new high and drops back, forming the left shoulder high; prices run up again to a new higher high before dropping back again, forming the head; then the market climbs to a high that is at about the same level as the left shoulder high before once again declining, forming the right shoulder. The key point of this pattern is the "neckline" or the roughly horizontal line that connects the two interim lows on the chart. (See Figure 3.17)

When prices drop below the neckline, the topping pattern is complete, and the market is likely to move into a new trend to the downside. However, as often happens at trend line penetrations or at breakout points, the market tends to come back to test the original move and may trade sideways for a while before deciding what it wants to do

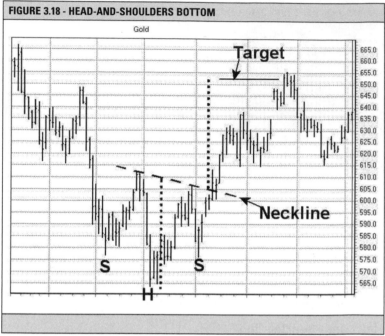

FIGURE 3.18 - HEAD-AND-SHOULDERS BOTTOM

Gold

Target

Neckline

S   S

H

VANTAGEPOINT INTERMARKET ANALYSIS SOFTWARE

next; so, the potential beginning of a downtrend may not be evident immediately. When prices do break below the neckline, the break sometimes occurs as a gap or with a strong move down, reinforcing the price reversal.

The head-and-shoulders formation is like some other patterns in that it can also be used as a measuring tool to project a price target. In traditional chart analysis, the distance from the top of the head to the neckline can be used to project the distance that the market will move from the neckline breakout point to a downside price target.

Head-and-shoulders Bottom

Just as the double bottom mirrors the double top, the head-and-shoulders bottom is like the head-and-shoulders top but in reverse. That is, prices slide to a low (left shoulder low), rally to an interim high, then fall back to a lower low (head), move back up, then sink again to a low at approximately the same level as the left shoulder low (right shoulder). (See Figure 3.18)

The neckline again is an important point. When prices break above the neckline, the reversal pattern is complete and a potential uptrend may begin. As with the head-and-shoulders top, there is likely to be some trading back and forth on either side of the neckline as the market makes its decision on which way to go, and the distance between the neckline and the head can be used to project how high prices might go.

Wedge

The wedge is basically a triangle formation or a variation of a trend channel that can be either a reversal or continuation pattern. Wedges usually form against the prevailing trend with a noticeable slant, and a breakout tends to occur in the direction of the main trend. In a falling wedge, the market is in an uptrend, but the highs are declining while buyers provide enough support to keep the market from tumbling. Eventually, the pressure from selling subsides, and buyers are able to push prices through the upper trend line. Although falling might suggest bearishness, a falling wedge is generally a bullish formation. (See Figure 3.19)

A rising wedge occurs when the market is in an overall price downtrend. Buyers continue to provide the force that pushes the lows above the previous lows, but highs are comparatively unchanged as selling pressure is sufficient to keep prices from taking off higher. Eventually, the lift from buying dries up and sellers take over, pushing prices below the short-term wedge uptrend line. A rising wedge is usually bearish.

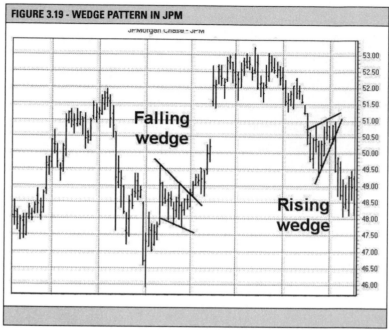

FIGURE 3.19 - WEDGE PATTERN IN JPM

VANTAGEPOINT INTERMARKET ANALYSIS SOFTWARE

The reverse of the wedge is a broadening formation that looks like a foghorn, generally signaling a reversal but a difficult pattern to trade because the widening price ranges take away the ability to see any trends.

These are some, but not all, of the major chart patterns that traders find useful for depicting market action and determining the price trend. A number of textbooks and web sites are available for the trader who wants to get a more in-depth study of chart patterns and analysis. Although some technical analysts rely only on chart patterns, that is not enough for others who want more quantitative measures of the direction and strength or weakness of market trends. To get more evidence to support their trading decisions, they like to use (single-market) price data to produce technical indicators that can provide even more insight into future price action.

Chapter 4

TECHNICAL INDICATORS:
ENHANCING PRICE PATTERNS

Identifying patterns and trends on a chart involves looking directly at prices—the open, high, low, and close for a given period. Instead of just a series of numbers, a chart presents price action in a more visually friendly manner, no matter what type of chart you use.

However, in an effort to get ahead of the crowd, some traders like to take their analysis of price data a little further, massaging the data through the use of various mathematical studies to produce a series of displays collectively known as technical indicators. Theses indicators are one step removed from examining prices directly on a chart but provide useful insights about the tone or strength of market moves. Although chart patterns can be quite subjective, indicators provide a specific, definable point at which to take action and are, therefore, quite useful in developing formal trading strategies as well as removing emotions from the trading decision process.

PREDICTIVE NATURE

Indicators generally attempt to be predictive—that is, they are intended to help the trader interpret market strength or weakness and indicate what prices might do in the future, as their name implies. Many imply only a trend direction for a market, much like the penetration of a trend line or other support or resistance area on a chart suggests.

Other indicators point to specific price or time targets, supporting some of the chart patterns described in the previous chapter, as they try to anticipate shifts in underlying market conditions. The types of indicators that try to pinpoint future price or time objectives include Elliott Wave, which features a five-wave sequence projecting the size and duration of market moves to arrive at specific price targets; Fibonacci levels, which provide retracement and extension targets based on a mathematical series of numbers and ratios; and cycles or seasonals, which identify the repetitive price movements of a market and project the timing of price highs or lows but not necessarily the amplitude of a move.

These indicators assume that the driving force behind price movement is the collective emotions of all market participants and that these emotions unfold in one of a series of patterns—that is, however traders have reacted to market conditions in the past is how they are likely to react again in the future, based on the mood of market participants and not necessarily supply/demand fundamentals.

Other types of indicators portray market sentiment and the composite action of the mass of market participants in hindsight, indicating the intensity of market opinion at a given price. These indicators include volume and open interest, which tend to reinforce whatever price action has taken place to validate a chart pattern; put/call ratios or advance/decline statistics for the stock market; or the Commitments of Traders report for the futures markets, which reveals the total positions of commercials, large speculators, and individual traders with the premise that the commercials are usually on the "right" side of the market.

Out of these readings of trading activity has come a class of analysis generally described as contrary opinion. Various services conduct surveys of traders, newsletter editors, or some other segment of the market to find out how many are bullish or bearish at current price levels. Briefly, the rationale is that if a large number of survey participants are bullish, they already have long positions so there is little buying power left; if a large percentage are bearish, they are already short so there is little selling pressure remaining. The best strategy in this case is to go contrary to the crowd's belief about market direction when you see these sentiment indicators.

Yet another type of indicator measures the volatility or the size of price fluctuations during a selected period. Changes in volatility usually lead changes in price. The Volatility Index (VIX) is an example of this type of indicator.

TRENDING VERSUS MOMENTUM

The most popular types of technical indicators included in many trading software packages are indicators that can be categorized further as trend-following indicators or momentum oscillators. Trend lines, moving averages, and moving average convergence/divergence (better known as MACD) are in the trending category, smoothing out price data to provide a general composite view of market direction. As their name suggests, they tend to perform well in trending markets.

Momentum indicators provide a measure of the speed at which prices move over a given time, indicating the strength or weakness of a trend as it progresses. They indicate when a price move may be running out of steam or is likely to make a reversal; as it inevitably will because no market goes up or down forever. These indicators generally oscillate on a scale between 0 and 100 and, as their name suggests, work best in choppy market conditions.

In many cases, it is not just the indicator reading that is significant but whether the pattern of indicator movement diverges from price movement. Examples of this type of indicator include stochastics and relative strength index (usually known as RSI) described below.

It would be impossible to include a discussion of every indicator in this book as there are literally hundreds of variations and even more ideas on how to apply them in trading. This chapter will focus on only a few of the major indicators. For more details on these indicators and many others, you should see a reference work such as **Technical Analysis of the Financial Markets** by John J. Murphy. Also note that some of our chart examples use predicted indicators, which will be explained in more detail later.

MOVING AVERAGES

As we have already emphasized, trend lines are the basic indicator of a trend, but where these trend lines are placed can be quite subjective, depending on what the trader "sees." The same is true for flags, triangles, or any other chart pattern that the trader identifies. Therefore, analysts have developed a number of technical indicators to quantify the data and smooth out the bar-to-bar fluctuations to provide a quantitative, non-subjective view of price direction.

The simplest, most reliable and most widely used technical indicator is a moving average, which uses the price data from a select number of prior time periods to filter out the random market "noise" and produce one composite number that can help traders see where the current price is relative to the average price for the selected number of periods. Moving averages help you spot market direction over time and keep you from being caught up in short-term erratic market fluctuations based on the latest price alone. There are many types of moving averages, with different characteristics. But one thing they all have in common, due to the way in which moving averages are calculated, are that they tend to lag behind the market.

A simple moving average is the average of a price series over a selected time period and gives an equal weight to each price during the period. You just add up the prices and divide by the number of prices to get the average. As a new price becomes available, it is added to the price series and the oldest price is dropped from the calculation, which allows the average to move over time. (See Figure 4.1)

FIGURE 4.1 - BRITISH POUND/ U.S. DOLLAR CHART

British Pound / U.S. Dollar

10-day simple moving average

10-day Simple Moving Average

VANTAGEPOINT INTERMARKET ANALYSIS SOFTWARE

A weighted moving average gives more weight to the latest prices because they logically are more important to the current situation than the older prices. For example, with a three-day weighted moving average, the latest price might be multiplied by three, the previous period's price by two, and the oldest price three periods ago by one. The sum of these figures is divided by the sum of the weighting factors—six in this example. This moving average is more responsive to current price changes.

An exponential moving average (EMA) is another form of a weighted moving average that gives more importance to the most recent prices, but retains all past prices in the series of prices used to calculate the average rather than dropping off the oldest prices. The current EMA is calculated by subtracting yesterday's EMA from today's price and then adding this result to yesterday's EMA to get today's EMA. An EMA line that carries at least a slight influence of all previous prices is generally smoother than other forms of moving averages. That can make a big difference in choppy market conditions.

In an attempt to overcome the lag effect of moving averages where the average trails behind the current price action, sometimes dramatically, some traders use a **displaced moving average**. Normally, a moving average for a given day is placed on a chart on the same day as the price data for that day, so the two are in alignment. A displaced moving average attempts to minimize the lag by "displacing" or "shifting" the moving average value forward in time on the chart.

For example, instead of putting a 5-day moving average value calculated for today in alignment with the price data for today on a chart, the average is plotted several days into the future on the chart. The premise behind displacing a moving average is that the future period's actual moving average value, which, of course, is not yet known, will turn out to be equal to today's actual moving average. This is a "forecast" of sorts but it is really just a guess of the future period's moving average value because you don't yet have the prices you need to compute that moving average value.

MULTIPLE VARIATIONS AND USES

Whatever moving average you use, the closing price for a period is typically used in making the calculation, but you can also use the open, high, or low or some combination of some or all of them.

The strategies used to employ moving averages in trading are also rather basic. They can be as simple as buy if the current price is above the moving average or sell if the current price is below the moving average. Or they may involve liquidating a position when the current price crosses below (or above) the moving average or reversing a position from long to short or vice versa. Or the moving average line may be treated as support or resistance such as the 50-day and 200-day moving averages that many stock market analysts continue to monitor.

Many traders use combinations of moving averages in crossover trading strategies. A buy signal occurs when the short-term moving average crosses from below to above a long-term average. A sell signal occurs when the short-term moving average crosses from above to below the long-term average.

In some cases, traders use a combination of three moving averages, such as 4-day, 9-day, and 18-day or 5-day, 10-day, and 20-day moving averages. When the shortest moving average is above the intermediate-term moving average and the intermediate average is above the longest moving average, you should be long and vice versa for a short position. (See Figure 4.2)

Other traders use the moving average lines, especially the longer-term averages, as a form of support or resistance. If prices have been above the moving average and then dip down to the moving average, they assume prices will recover and bounce up from the moving average line so they buy rather than expect a crossover and a sell signal.

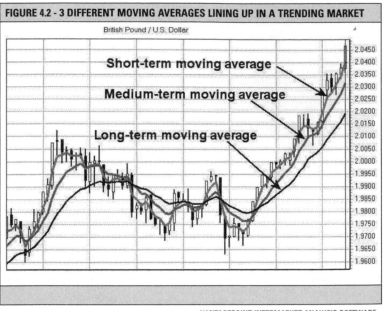

FIGURE 4.2 - 3 DIFFERENT MOVING AVERAGES LINING UP IN A TRENDING MARKET

British Pound / U.S. Dollar

Short-term moving average

Medium-term moving average

Long-term moving average

VANTAGEPOINT INTERMARKET ANALYSIS SOFTWARE

By their very nature, moving averages are changing all the time as each new price gets factored into the equation. With today's personal computer power, some traders test all kinds of time frames or combinations to find the optimal moving averages, sometimes changing their size frequently (and perhaps even too frequently) or having different moving average parameters for each stock or futures market in a seemingly futile attempt to keep up with constantly changing market conditions.

The danger is that they will over-optimize and curve-fit the data to a particular market and/or time frame and then become disappointed if the new parameters don't perform the same in actual trading as they did during their testing period.

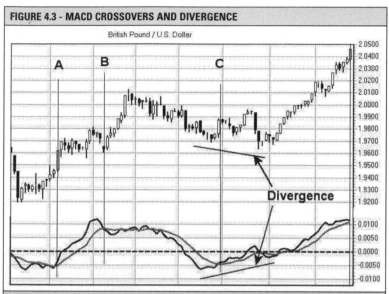

FIGURE 4.3 - MACD CROSSOVERS AND DIVERGENCE

British Pound / U.S. Dollar

Crossovers of the predicted MACD and the MACD trigger provide confirming signals at vertical lines A, B and C. However, B turns out to be a false sell signal as MACD stays at the upper end of its scale for days, one of the weaknesses of these types of indicators. On the other hand, divergence – prices falling, MACD rising – provides a good indication of underlying price strength.

VANTAGEPOINT INTERMARKET ANALYSIS SOFTWARE

MOVING AVERAGE CONVERGENCE DIVERGENCE (MACD)

MACD uses moving averages but adds several concepts to the standard crossover techniques of moving averages to provide potential trading signals for market changes. MACD plots the difference between a long-term exponential moving average (often 26 days) and a short-term exponential moving average (often 12 days) and then compares this line to an exponential moving average (often 9 days) of this difference, which is generally used as a trigger line.

Crossovers of the two lines themselves provide trading signals. When the MACD line crosses below the trigger line, it is a bearish signal; when the MACD line crosses above the trigger line, it is a bullish indication. Crossing above or below a zero line can also be used as a signal because it suggests the strength or weakness of a market. (See Figure 4.3)

The relationship of the MACD line and the trigger line also offers trading signals. If the MACD line pulls away from the trigger line dramatically, it indicates the market may be becoming overbought or oversold after a strong move and is likely due for a correction that will bring the two lines back together to a more normal position.

One of the major uses of MACD, as with a number of other indicators, is to identify divergence between actual prices and the indicator. If the MACD turns positive and makes higher lows while prices are still moving lower, this could be a strong buy signal, as MACD detects strength that is not yet evident on the price chart. If the MACD makes lower highs while prices are reaching new highs, this bearish divergence suggests a sell signal.

With its moving average base, MACD is a lagging indicator and prices usually have to make a rather strong move to generate a signal. Like moving averages, MACD tends to work best in markets that make broad trending moves and does not perform as well under choppy, congested trading conditions.

STOCHASTICS

The premise of the stochastic indicator is based on the position of the current price relative to the price range during a specified period. Developers of stochastics observed that, when prices are declining, daily closes tend to accumulate near the extreme lows of the day and

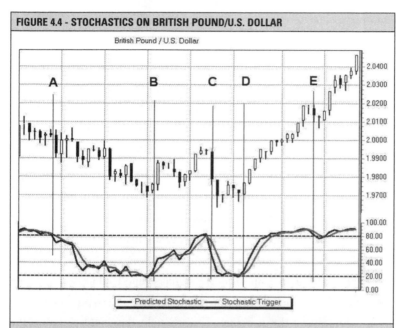

FIGURE 4.4 - STOCHASTICS ON BRITISH POUND/U.S. DOLLAR

British Pound / U.S. Dollar

The stochastics indicator signals a long position when predicted stochastics is near or below 20 and crosses above the stochastics trigger. A sell signal occurs on a crossover down from near or above 80 on the stochastics scale. Note at vertical line E the stochastics indicator is not much help when the market is trending higher.

VANTAGEPOINT INTERMARKET ANALYSIS SOFTWARE

that, when prices are in a rising mode, closes tend to cluster toward the extreme highs of the day. The stochastic oscillator is designed to use these price tendencies to indicate oversold and overbought market conditions. (See Figure 4.4)

Stochastics are measured and represented by two components, %K and %D. The %K line—the faster, more sensitive indicator—is calculated by taking the close minus the low for N periods and dividing that number by the high minus the low for N periods and then multiplying the result by 100. This puts the final figure on a scale ranging from 0 to 100. Some traders prefer slow stochastics, a line produced by calculating a short-term moving average of the %K line. The %D line is a longer-term moving average of the %K value.

A high stochastics value—usually above 70 or 80—indicates the market is overbought; a low stochastics reading—usually below 20 or 30—indicates the market is oversold. When the %K line crosses the slower-moving %D line in overbought or oversold territory, this suggests a market may be about to reverse direction.

One of the shortcomings of the stochastic indicator, as well as other indicators of its type, is that once it indicates an overbought or oversold situation, it can't tell you how much further the market might move in its current direction. It may continue to show a signal for days or weeks at a time if the market is in a trending condition. To reduce the chances for acting on an early signal, some traders require both the %K and %D lines to be pointing in the direction of predicted price move while above the designated overbought threshold or below the oversold level.

As with other indicators, one of the most important signals with stochastics is divergence between %D and price, which occurs when the %D line makes a series of lower highs while prices make a series of higher highs, or the %D line makes a series of higher lows while prices are making a series of lower lows. This may not be an immediate call to action but suggests you need to be alert for a market signal because the underlying tone of the market is changing.

RELATIVE STRENGTH INDEX (RSI)

In some cases, a sharp price movement from the past may have a profound effect on a momentum indicator and cause it to flash false signals, even though recent prices have been relatively stable. In addition, an overbought or oversold level for one market may not be

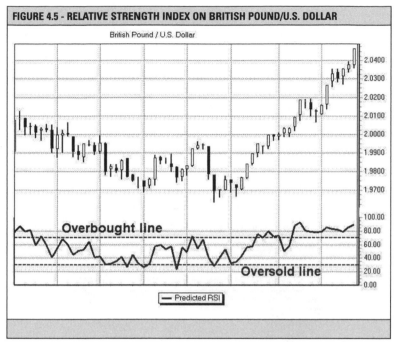

FIGURE 4.5 - RELATIVE STRENGTH INDEX ON BRITISH POUND/U.S. DOLLAR

British Pound / U.S. Dollar

Overbought line

Oversold line

— Predicted RSI

VANTAGEPOINT INTERMARKET ANALYSIS SOFTWARE

the same for some other market, and the way you read and use the momentum data may need to be adjusted.

The Relative Strength Index (RSI) is designed to smooth out these sharp fluctuations in price movement to provide a measure of market strength or weakness on a constant scale ranging from 0 to 100. (See Figure 4.5)

To calculate RSI, figure out the average of the up closes and the average of the down closes for a given period (typically 14 days), then divide the average of the up closes by the average of the down closes to get a relative strength figure. Add 1 to that relative strength figure, divide the sum into 100, and subtract that result from 100 to get the index reading. (It may sound complicated, but most analytical software programs do all that calculating for you in an instant.)

As with other indicators, a low RSI figure—usually below 30—implies a market that is oversold or the potential for a weakening bear market; a high RSI reading—typically above 70—suggests an overbought condition or the potential for a weakening bull market. A move to those levels is not an automatic buy or sell signal but just suggests that market conditions may be ripe for a market bottom or top. You should have corroboration from some other technique or indicators before acting on the signal.

Also, as with other indicators, divergence between the direction of RSI and price may be the best use for RSI—for example, when prices reach new highs after a bull market setback but the RSI fails to exceed its previous highs.

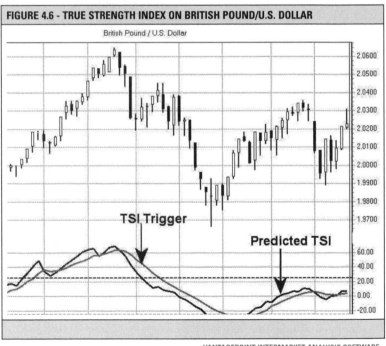

FIGURE 4.6 - TRUE STRENGTH INDEX ON BRITISH POUND/U.S. DOLLAR

British Pound / U.S. Dollar

TSI Trigger

Predicted TSI

VANTAGEPOINT INTERMARKET ANALYSIS SOFTWARE

TRUE STRENGTH INDEX (TSI)

The True Strength Index is another momentum oscillator, but it tends to reflect smoother changes in its readings because it double smoothes momentum values (the difference in price between one period and the next) by using two moving averages. The price differences, or momentum, act as a proxy for price and its values are more sensitive than just using price. These values are then slowed down by using two smoothing moving averages.

As a result, TSI more closely aligns with price highs and lows in defining a market trend and doesn't look as erratic as other indicators such as MACD. Buying or selling signals occur when the TSI crosses above or below the TSI signal line. TSI signals can be especially useful for identifying divergence between two related markets such as comparing two stock indexes to each other. (See Figure 4.6)

INDICATOR DEFICIENCIES

No matter which of these indicators you use or how many variations you have for them, these indicators do have some general limitations, which have a serious impact on trading performance:

Most technical indicators are based on one thing, price. With price as the core input, many indicators tend to be just another rendition of what some other indicator already shows and do not provide different information.

Prices used in most indicators all occurred in the past so most indicators lag or trail behind current market action. In fast-moving markets, where the price is on the verge of rising sharply or falling precipitously, this lag effect can be very pronounced and costly because of the delay in indicator response.

Because of this lag effect, an indicator may work well in some market conditions but not in others. For example, a moving average works well in trending situations but poorly when the market moves sideways or chops back and forth. A momentum indicator such as stochastics works better in these choppier conditions but does not do so well in extended trending markets. Because you cannot determine exactly which market condition will exist in the future, you cannot rely on just one type of indicator. One magic indicator that fits all markets is not a realistic expectation.

- With different types of market conditions and different indicators, indicators are unlikely to get you into or out of a position exactly at the top or bottom. The best you can hope to do is capture part of a move and hope that part is significant enough to provide sufficient profits to justify the risk you have to take to get into the position. If you rely on most traditional indicators, you generally will be giving up a lot of potential profits before market conditions become clear, but that's the nature of these types of indicators.

- You can make countless adjustments to an indicator, but you can never make it perfect. For example, the shorter the length of a moving average, the more sensitive it will be to short-term price fluctuations, meaning less lag than longer moving averages; but, the price you pay is less effective in smoothing or filtering out market "noise."

- Indicators can generate false signals that can chew up your account with whipsaw losses. A moving average, for example, may provide several crossover signals that get you in and out of positions a number of times before giving you a valid signal at the beginning of a longer-term trend.

This is not conducive to giving you confidence to trade, and you may give up on an indicator right before it gives a valid signal.

Even with their limitations, popular indicators like moving averages are important quantitative tools to help traders identify trends and determine when changes in trend direction have occurred. The lag effect in indicators has presented the biggest challenge that technical analysts and traders (myself included) have been trying to overcome for years. Extensive research has been directed at finding ways to reduce the lag, while at the same time retaining the benefits of these indicators.

Some trading strategies attempt to reduce the lag by comparing an actual price, such as the daily close, with an indicator to determine trends. Other strategies attempt to minimize whipsaws by using multiple indicators. The number of permutations and combinations that can go into perfecting an indicator's characteristics is staggering.

Yet, the essential problem remains with most indicators: Almost everything depends on past prices, and the lag effect from using this old information is often not very useful in forecasting future price action. In short, while a picture of the past provides some analytical basis for action, most traders are more interested in the picture for the future. They want some idea about what is likely to happen tomorrow.

Although it is impossible to overcome completely this dependency on past prices, my research since the mid-1980s (when I first began developing intermarket-based indicators that could lead the market) has revealed a way to analyze price data that can be more useful. It doesn't eliminate all of the deficiencies of indicators, but it can give you an edge in forecasting trends and possible reversals. And a little edge is often all a trader needs to be successful.

Chapter 5

USING INTERMARKET
ANALYSIS TO GAIN AN EDGE

Despite the limitations described in the previous chapter, technical indicators continue to be widely used by traders. Moving averages, in particular, are highly recognized in the financial industry as an important quantitative trend identification tool. At the same time, however, the inherent lagging nature of moving averages continues to be a serious shortcoming. If this deficiency were to be overcome somehow, moving averages could be transformed into one of the most effective trend identification and forecasting indicators in financial market analysis.

As outlined in the previous chapter, traditional moving averages are computed using only past price data, so turning points in moving averages will always lag behind turning points in prices and, therefore, fall short as predictive indicators of what is likely to happen in the market. When you are trying to figure out what the market direction will be in order to set your entry or exit point, any lag, however small, can be financially ruinous, especially given today's market volatility.

TAPPING A DIFFERENT DATA STREAM

That realization sent me on a research mission more than two decades ago to see if I could find some way to retain the positive attributes of moving averages while overcoming their limitations—namely, their lagging nature. After years of studying the markets, observing the transition to global markets and developing countless computerized trading strategies, I began formulating an approach in the mid-1980s that explored the markets from an intermarket perspective. By incorporating the influence of market data from closely related markets in conjunction with price data from a target market, I was able to create quantitative indicators that no longer relied only on past price data for the target market alone but incorporated the effects of related markets.

Past price data for the target market are still an essential component of this analysis, but when combined with price data from related markets, innovative technical indicators can be developed that produce superior analytics when compared to traditional technical analysis indicators or studies using only single-market data. Intermarket data helps transform lagging indicators into leading indicators that can be used to forecast expected changes in market trend direction within a short time span of a day or two into the future with a relatively high degree of accuracy.

Of course, the further you try to look into the future, the less reliable the forecast. Weather forecasters trying to predict the weather for the next six months or a year have a rather spotty record because so many random and unforeseen events can happen to alter weather patterns. In recent years, however, weather forecasters using more advanced forecasting tools have developed a good record for predicting the weather for the next few days.

The same thing is true in trading. It's impossible to say where the price of crude oil or any other market will be six months or a year from now with any degree of precision. That's why I have limited the time horizon for forecasting markets to the next few days. Even being able to anticipate price action for a day ahead is still more than enough lead time to provide a trader with a tremendous trading advantage over the masses who still rely only on single-market, lagging indicators.

Unfortunately, you can never be 100% accurate when it comes to forecasting market direction or prices for even one day in advance. No one will ever achieve perfection in predicting financial markets.

WHY INTERMARKET ANALYSIS?

Before the mid-1980s when each country's domestic markets tended to trade in their own little world, the markets were less volatile and single-market methods were sufficient for technical analysis. With today's rapid global communications and highly interdependent global markets, a narrow view that looks only at the internal dynamics of each individual market is much too limited. With the speed of electronic trading around the clock amid the dynamics of global trading, traders need to expand their perspective and take into consideration external factors that affect every market.

If you were a licensed pilot preparing to fly your private plane from New York City to Washington, D.C. just before dusk one summer evening, you would certainly check everything on your preflight checklist to be sure that all of the plane's internal operating systems were functioning properly—the visual fuel and oil gauges, control movements, altimeter, compasses, flaps, mags, engine runup, and all of the other elements essential for your plane to operate safely.

You would almost certainly also inquire about one critical external factor: the weather outlook for your flight path. If you ignore this external environmental context in which your plane will be flying, you are implicitly assuming that either the weather conditions will be favorable or will not affect your flight adversely. As many experienced pilots will tell you, if the weather conditions become unfavorable for flight, it can be a life or death decision.

> **Ignorance is not bliss when it comes to piloting planes or trading futures, forex, or equities in today's global markets.**

Trading Treasury bonds, crude oil, the S&P 500 Index, or the Japanese yen is no different if you ignore the broader intermarket forces affecting these individual markets. Ignorance is not bliss when it comes to piloting planes or trading futures, forex, or equities in today's global markets. If you have the right tools, which can give you pertinent information, you will be able to make sound, calculated decisions; if you don't, you are just gambling, either with your life or with your hard-earned money.

Obviously, you still have to analyze the behavior of each individual market because your actual positions will be in those markets. And, naturally, you'll want to identify the failed double tops, broken trend lines, and price moves above or below their 50-day or 200-day moving averages. These are still useful indicators of market direction, if for no other reason than the fact that they are followed by so many other traders who act on the patterns that are easy to spot. This produces market movements resulting from the mass psychology of all of the traders engaged in trading a particular market.

However, it is not good enough to look only at each individual market by itself with popular single-market indicators that look retrospectively at an individual market's past data in an effort to identify reoccurring patterns that can then be extrapolated into the future. This type of analysis really boils down to relying on where the market has been in the past to try and discover where it is going to go in the future.

I prefer to forecast market direction prospectively in a manner that captures the character and nature of today's globally interdependent financial markets. This can be accomplished by using intermarket analysis tools comprised of leading indicators that can tell you whether an existing trend is likely to continue or is about to change direction, taking a lot of the guesswork out of trading.

INTERMARKET ANALYSIS IN EQUITIES

Intermarket analysis is not new by any means. It has roots in both the equity and commodity markets. Historically, equity traders have looked at relationships among individual stocks, sectors, and broad market indexes. They have also made comparisons between the debt and equity markets, as the effects of fluctuating interest rates, inflationary expectations, and central bank policies have played an increasingly important role in determining the market direction of equities. More recently, traders have compared broad market indexes representing various stock markets around the world to see where the best opportunities are.

Here are some areas of intermarket analysis within the equity markets that should come as no surprise to you:

- Domestic broad market indexes to one another.

- Domestic stock indexes to similar market indexes in other countries such as the Nikkei 225 and FTSE 100.

- Market sectors to the broad market indexes.

- Individual stocks to broad market indexes.

- Individual stocks to one another within a sector.

- Relationship of price, time, and volume to one another.

- Comparing indicators such as advance/decline to the performance of broad market indexes.

- Analyzing movements in interest rates to movements in stock indexes such as the relationship between 10-year Treasury notes and the S&P 500 Index.

INTERMARKET ANALYSIS IN FUTURES AND COMMODITIES

By their nature, futures and commodity markets, including currencies, have historically lent themselves to intermarket analysis. With both a cash market and numerous futures contract months existing simultaneously for a given market, it is natural for traders to make comparisons between markets or between contracts representing different expirations. In addition, many market complexes have closely related markets or contracts within them, whether it is the grains, meats, currencies, interest rates, stock indexes, metals, or energies. Because of this, intramarket and intermarket spread analysis has become an integral part of technical analysis today and in the future.

Here are just some of the spreads between futures markets of related instruments that traders watch to gain additional insight into market direction:

- Notes over bonds—more commonly known as the "NOB" spread—the spread between 10-year Treasury notes and 30-year Treasury bonds.

- T-bills vs. Eurodollars—the "TED" spread—between 90-day Treasury bills and the 90-day Eurodollar.

- Bonds vs. a host of other markets such as commodity price indexes, the U.S. Dollar Index, gold, crude oil, and others.

- Wheat vs. corn.

- Cattle vs. hogs.

- Soybeans vs. soybean meal and/or soybean oil.

- Crude oil vs. heating oil.

In short, almost every area where one product might substitute for another product or where a valid competitive relationship exists between two markets is a ripe trading ground for spread traders and intermarket analysis. Exchanges have long recognized these relationships between markets with established performance bond rates for the most closely connected and popular spread trades. Traders in a market on one side of a spread cannot afford to ignore what is happening to the market on the other side of the spread. Forex pairs, a popular new product that has attracted the attention of traders all over the world, is really nothing new. It combines two related currencies into a structured spread trade, which is identical to the concept of spreading individual currency futures against one another, which has been done for decades.

FUTURES, EQUITIES TIED TOGETHER

Intermarket comparisons between futures and the equity markets highlight short-term confirmation or divergence, which provides insight into impending changes in market trend direction. Traders can monitor futures as an early barometer of what might happen in the equity markets. Futures on the S&P 500 Index, the DOW, Treasury bonds/

notes, and other financial futures markets and commodities (such as crude oil or various commodity price indexes) are often mentioned as having strong influences on the equity markets as traders recognize the relationships between the two instruments.

Higher commodity price indexes, for example, suggest higher inflation rates in the future, tending to drive Treasury note prices lower (and interest rates higher). This connection is also negative for those sectors of the equity markets linked to commodities including the agricultural, banking, energy, metals, and industrials sectors.

Globally related markets, responding to various global and domestic economic considerations, can be analyzed with respect to their confirmation or divergence from one another. For instance, changes in short-term interest rates enacted by the U.S. Federal Reserve Board, the European Central Bank, Bank of England, or the Bank of Japan can have a significant effect on foreign currency futures or the forex market, depending on interest rate differentials. Global arbitrage of interest rates tends to keep international debt markets synchronized.

Every market, both domestically and internationally, now appears to have some effect on every other market, however seemingly distant and unrelated. A thorough analysis of the outlook of any one market is now incomplete without looking at it within a broad intermarket context.

MARKET LEADS AND LAGS

Although direct and inverse relationships may appear to link markets to one another on the surface when they are examined two at a time, these linkages are neither fixed nor linear in nature. Instead, they are dynamic and have varying strengths as well as varying leads and lags to one another that shift over time.

With the increased emphasis lately on 24-hour electronic trading, traders often expect the effects of one market on a related market to be instantaneous and linear. They think that all they have to do is look at what Treasury bonds or notes are doing at any moment to get clues about what the stock market will do next. Unfortunately for them, this is not how the financial markets work. Sometimes cause and effect may be reversed, with stocks seeming to lead bonds and notes, but at other times the Treasury contracts appear to lead stocks.

The interrelationships of markets have become even more pronounced as the markets have become increasingly globalized. Despite the importance of analyzing intermarket relationships in this context, many traders are still too preoccupied with looking inward at each market, ignoring the interdependencies of the financial markets and their effects on one another.

In addition, technical analysts and traders have made little progress at objectively (quantitatively), not just subjectively (qualitatively), identifying repetitive patterns in market data, which is a necessary step for effective forecasting.

It is now imperative for traders to adopt an intermarket perspective and to incorporate intermarket analysis into their trading strategies so they can deal with the global financial markets as they really exist.

If you look at the planet Saturn through an inexpensive, low-powered telescope, you won't see the rings that surround it. They are there, but the tool you are using doesn't have the capability to see them. The same is true for how you look at the markets. Although the interconnections are there, depending on the approach you use and its limitations, you may not see them. But you can bet that other sophisticated traders do. Failing to factor the linkages between related markets in their trading strategies no doubt contributes to the financial fatality rate among traders, especially novices.

EARLY INTERMARKET ANALYSIS FAILURES

Because of the complexity of the dynamic interactions among financial markets, it is difficult for the beginning trader to perform even rudimentary intermarket analysis. To overcome this obstacle, technical analysts have devised various means to accomplish what is commonly described as intermarket analysis. Here are three popular, yet in my opinion deficient, ways that novice traders and others attempt to quantify the effects of related markets:

- Comparing price charts on two markets to one another, calculating the difference between the two markets' prices on a minute-by-minute, hourly, daily, weekly, or monthly basis and presenting the data graphically or numerically as an indication of future market direction.

- Calculating a ratio of prices representing two markets and presenting the information graphically or numerically to show how the two markets have behaved relative to one another in the past to help anticipate what they are likely to do in the future.

- Performing a statistical linear correlation analysis on two markets to measure the degree to which the prices of one market move in relation to the prices of the second market. The mathematical indicator used to measure correlation is known as a statistical correlation coefficient.

The problem with the first two approaches is that historically "normal" differences or ratios can be breeched. If you've ever traded currency spreads or forex pairs, you know what I mean. When these differences or ratios go against you, you quickly discover that spreading or trading forex can be very risky (even more so than trading outright commodity or futures contracts) as you get hammered on both sides of the spread or forex pair.

As the number of markets to explore from an intermarket perspective increases, the ineffectiveness of these methods becomes more pronounced. These methods of analyzing intermarket relationships are limited to comparing prices of only two markets at a time, often assuming incorrectly that the effects of one market on another occur without any leads or lags. In addition, methods such as linear correlation analysis presuppose the effects are linear in nature in a sort of one-to-one causal relationship. This, too, is unrealistic when it comes to how the global financial markets really function.

Leads and lags exist between domestic and international economic activity and the financial markets and between related domestic and global financial markets. Sometimes the effects may not be discernible for days, weeks, or months, as in the case of inflationary pressures on a variety of markets or the implementation of central bank monetary policies that take time to work their way through the global economy.

To examine effectively the combined simultaneous effects of as few as five or ten related markets on a target market, methods such as linear correlation analysis and subjective chart pattern analysis are totally inadequate as market forecasting tools.

IMPROVING YOUR VISION

Most traders find it just too difficult and time-consuming to keep up with more than two or three related markets simultaneously to figure out how they influence each other. It is relatively easy to "eyeball" two or three charts at the same time or to perform a linear correlation between two markets at a time. However, these approaches fail to capture the simultaneous combined effects of numerous related markets on a specific target market.

Put a hand over one of your eyes and try walking around the room. With only one eye open, your field of vision is limited and your ability to visualize your surroundings is severely restricted. Next, drop your hand and walk around the room with both eyes open. Now you are really benefiting from your full field of vision.

This gives you a sense of the difference between single-market analysis and intermarket analysis. Most traders make their trading decisions with a narrow, one-eyed focus on each market in isolation. Don't you think you would be better off if you tackle your trading with both eyes wide open?

Traders who continue to limit themselves to single-market analysis and rely upon lagging indicators to determine market direction are confronted with a similar situation. What they are doing is not wrong; it's just not adequate, given the complexities of today's globally interconnected markets.

BEEFING UP WITH INTERMARKET ANALYSIS

Let me emphasize again that you do not have to stop performing market-by-market technical analysis or to abandon the use of trend-following methods that have played a key role in technical analysis for decades. Many popular single-market technical indicators are useful to one degree or another to analyze internal market behavior. All I am suggesting is that these sorts of analytical tools can be made more effective when used in combination with intermarket data. It will give

TABLE 5.1 - THE SCOPE OF INTERMARKET ANALYSIS

INTERMARKET ANALYSIS WITH TREND-FORECASTING INDICATORS	SINGLE-MARKET ANALYSIS WITH TREND-FOLLOWING INDICATORS
Looks at multiple markets simultaneously, analyzes their effect on a target market	Looks at one market at a time
Leads the market, pinpointing trading opportunities as they are about to unfold	Lags the market, causing traders to miss the start of new trends
Traders can enter and exit trades just as the trend is changing	Trades are often triggered several days after the trend has changed direction
Trends are identified as they are developing so traders catch a bigger portion of each move	Often gives back a large portion of profits, sometimes turning a profitable trade into a losing trade
Stops are placed based on how related markets are affecting the market being traded	Stop placements are determined by looking at the market being traded, often based on commonly used indicators such as trend lines, which tends to cluster stops near one another
False trading signals are minimized because the full picture is considered, not just a small piece of it	False signals are common during sideways markets, resulting in frequent losing trades

you a more comprehensive view of each target market from both an internal as well as an external perspective.

This is not an "either-or" choice. Intermarket analysis and trend forecasting approaches based upon it can be used as a confirmation to single-market, trend-following approaches. With this broader framework, you can much more effectively identify and avoid marginal trades because intermarket analysis builds upon the strengths of single-market analysis. By adding another dimension to the analytic framework, the behavior of each market can be analyzed both internally as well as within the broader intermarket context of today's global financial markets, as Table 5.1 depicts.

A more quantitative approach to implementing intermarket analysis, such as I advocate, is not a radical departure from traditional technical analysis nor is it an attempt to replace it. Intermarket analysis is simply the next logical developmental stage in the evolution of technical analysis when you recognize the global nature of today's interdependent, highly complex economies and integrated financial markets.

If you need to dig a hole in the ground, you wouldn't do it with a teaspoon. Similarly, if you want to stir a cup of coffee, you wouldn't use a spade. You would use the right tool for the job. Today's interdependent, interconnected, global financial markets require using the right tool if you really intend to be successful as a trader.

After reading my case for intermarket analysis, you may conclude, "Okay, I agree with you that intermarket analysis should be the basis for analyzing today's global markets, but if past prices of individual markets aren't the complete answer, what do I use for data? And where do I get this information?"

The next chapter provides my proposed solution on what the best way is to implement intermarket analysis. It is not 100 percent perfect—no approach to trading will ever achieve perfection, contrary to the hype you may hear. It is, however, a method that not only excels at finding reoccurring patterns and relationships between markets but also spots patterns within a single market that can be used to make highly accurate forecasts of market trend direction. These forecasts can help turn lagging indicators into leading indicators, putting probabilities on your side and improving your odds of becoming a more successful trader.

Chapter 6

MINING INTERMARKET
DATA WITH NEURAL NETWORKS

Unlike years ago when the global economy (and globalization of markets) first began taking shape, today you would have to be completely
isolated not to hear about globalization and how markets are affecting
each other daily, if not more often. Now, it would be hard to find a
trader who wouldn't agree that what happens in one market influences
what happens in other related markets. By analyzing the effects of
related markets—particularly futures markets, which are inherently
oriented toward anticipating future price levels—even novice traders
can find early warnings of impending changes in market direction.
These early warnings can be gleaned directly from watching key
related markets.

Although it is easy to recognize the value of intermarket analysis
intuitively, the big question is: how can an individual trader quantify
these relationships so that he or she can apply the resulting information to tradable opportunities?

If you had the next day's *Investor's Business Daily*® or *The Wall Street
Journal*® available to you every morning with your coffee—a one-day
lead on everyone else—it wouldn't take long to become one of the

wealthiest people in the world. With 100% accurate information about market activity the next day, you would know exactly what to expect and could trade accordingly.

If that is your dream for attaining trading success, you might as well forget about it because you aren't going to get tomorrow's newspaper delivered to your door one day in advance nor, unfortunately, will you ever find any other way to make 100% accurate forecasts of the financial markets. Forecasting, by its very nature, inherently involves mathematical probabilities, not certainty.

The good news, though, is that you do not have to have a market forecast that is perfect to tilt the odds in your favor. All you need to gain a substantial competitive advantage over other traders is a reasonably reliable forecast that can beat a coin toss consistently. Of course, the more accurate your forecast, the bigger your edge and the more successful you can be as the world's financial markets become increasingly interconnected.

PLAYING THE HAND YOU'RE DEALT

You have probably heard the expression in poker—and in life as well—that you have to play the hand that is dealt to you. So what are all traders dealt that they can use to make smart trading decisions?

We discussed earlier how supply and demand, weather forecasts, political and economic events, and many other fundamental factors provide the driving force for market action; but, unless you have a Ph.D. in economics or inside information, you probably are not going to be able to compete very well on this level.

What you do have are the results of the trading activity that these sophisticated, institutional traders and other market participants produce in the form of market price data. You may not have the high-speed connection they have or the capability to enter orders quite as quickly, but with today's Internet, telecommunications, and computing technologies you can come close if short-term, fast-paced trading is your style. The information lag that previously existed between the trading floor and off-floor speculators has been narrowed as electronic trading now allows prices to be disseminated widely and rapidly to a vast number of traders around the globe who all see the same prices that you do.

You also have volume and open interest data to consider, although that exchange-generated data may be delayed for the benefit of exchange members. You have position reports, such as the weekly Commitments of Traders (COT) reports compiled by the Commodity Futures Trading Commission, which are released several days after the positions are reported. Of course, you also have various sentiment readings, market commentaries, and opinions that are disseminated by analysts and bloggers on which you can base your trading decisions.

In truth, the only real piece of information you have to work with is the net effect of all these inputs, and that is price. As was emphasized earlier, the problem with past price data is that it has already occurred. Furthermore, everybody has access to historical price data, and they use many different techniques to massage old prices in an attempt to uncover new clues about future market strength and direction. Unfortunately, most traders who use these typical methods of analysis tend to lose money. It may not be the techniques they are using that are solely at fault; it may also be the limited, single-market data that they are feeding into their analysis.

ENTER INTERMARKET DATA

In the mid-1980s it became increasingly clear to me that the character and nature of the financial markets was beginning to undergo an inherent change. As the global economy began to take form, I knew intermarket analysis would become essential to traders who wanted to get an early reading on price direction in a target market ahead of the trading crowd. I realized quickly that widely used technical indicators (with which I was already very familiar) could be applied to intermarket analysis of global data in innovative ways by using an artificial intelligence tool known as a neural network to help make more accurate short-term trend forecasts.

Using extensive intermarket data and realizing that it would be impossible to make reliable price forecasts for more than a few days in the future (just like it is impossible to make long-term weather forecasts), I began researching and developing predictive indicators that could forecast the market direction for the next day or two and forewarn whether or not a target market is about to make a top or bottom shortly and change trend direction. This is all done automatically through the pattern recognition and forecasting capabilities of neural networks applied to intermarket data. Once the neural networks have been researched, properly designed, trained, and tested, they can be used in actual trading with current data updated each trading day to generate short-term trend forecasts for any chosen target market.

Almost anyone can look at a bar chart and tell you what the trend has been by looking at what happened to prices yesterday and over the last few days or weeks. Hindsight is 20/20, but you can't make money tomorrow or next week based on what happened yesterday or last week. You can only make money if you can anticipate, with reasonable accuracy on a consistent basis, what is likely to happen in the near future.

Applying neural networks to intermarket data to forecast moving averages and other commonly used technical indicators such as MACD, RSI, and Stochastics supercharges these indicators by transforming them from lagging into leading indicators. With a small time advantage of even just one day, you can put the probabilities on your side and gain an edge over other traders, which can make the difference between success and failure. Remember the cliché, "The early bird gets the worm."

ENTER NEURAL NETWORKS

Neural networks have been applied successfully to corporate decision-making (including risk analysis and fraud detection), character recognition, medical diagnostics, and many other areas for many years. When first applied to financial markets in the early 1990s, neural networks initially had their share of skeptics and detractors in the financial industry. This was the same reaction that greeted strategy back-testing and optimization when I introduced that capability into trading software for personal computers a decade earlier.

Software developers from outside of the financial industry, who were knowledgeable about neural networks applied to other arenas, perceived a potentially lucrative marketplace for their software among traders and flooded the financial industry with an assortment of neural network software programs for traders. By the mid-1990s neural networks were being hyped in promotional marketing literature as the Holy Grail of technical analysis and became the buzz word of the day as expectations about their potential reached dizzying heights.

Unfamiliar with the intricacies of the financial markets and the details underlying technical analysis, many of these newcomers to the financial industry helped foster a backlash against neural networks, as the so-called Holy Grail remained elusive.

My focus, though, since the mid-1980s has centered on the globalization of the markets and the application of intermarket analysis to global market data. Neural networks just happened to be an effective mathematical tool that I had identified for 1) discerning hidden patterns and relationships in seemingly disparate market data and 2) making reasonably accurate short-term market forecasts in a non-subjective, quantitative manner. Neural networks are not the magic bullet that they were hyped up to be. They are the means, not the end.

A MODEL OF THE HUMAN BRAIN

The human brain has hundreds of billions of cells known as neurons, which, through their connections to each other, relay information from one neuron to another. This process allows a person to learn relationships, draw inferences, recognize patterns, and make predictions, among other tasks. Although substantially less complex than the human brain, software-based artificial neural networks model how the human brain processes information and performs pattern recognition and forecasting.

Neural networks are excellent at sifting through enormous amounts of seemingly unrelated market data and finding repetitive patterns and nonlinear relationships that may exist between a target market and numerous related markets. These connections could never be perceived visually just by looking at price charts or by comparing two markets to one another. Through a mathematical error minimization process known as "learning" or "training," neural networks, if designed properly, can be trained to make highly accurate market forecasts based upon these hidden patterns.

Artificial neural networks are comprised of individual neurons organized in layers and interconnected through selected network architecture with variable mathematical weights attributed to each connection. Each target market is paired with a selected number of intermarkets, which most closely correlate with and influence the target market. Every market is tested as a potential intermarket for every other market, and the most influential intermarkets are selected for inclusion in the model. The architecture includes an input layer, hidden layer, and an output layer, as shown in Figure 6.1.

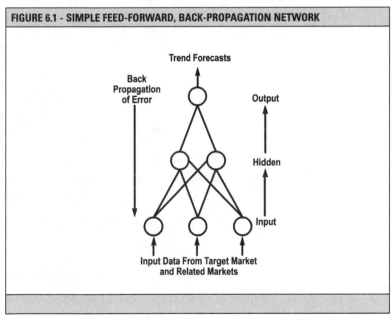

FIGURE 6.1 - SIMPLE FEED-FORWARD, BACK-PROPAGATION NETWORK

MARKET TECHNOLOGIES, LLC.

INPUT LAYER

A neural network is not limited to single-market technical data inputs but is excellent at applying intermarket data—and even fundamental data or other types of inputs—to market forecasting. The raw input data from the target market and related markets, the statistical "preprocessing" of the raw data, the network architecture, and the training and testing regimens can be custom-tailored to each target market.

For instance, for a neural network designed to forecast the price outlook for crude oil, the analysis might include five or ten years of past price, volume, and open interest data on crude oil futures as well as the 20 or 25 markets determined to be most closely correlated with crude oil. Once the raw input data has been selected, it is preprocessed using various algebraic and statistical methods of transformation to facilitate learning.

HIDDEN LAYER

The hidden layer is used by a neural network for internal processing in order to store its "intelligence" during the learning process. This layer is composed of neurons where the network recodes the input data into a form that captures hidden patterns and relationships. The network generalizes from previously learned facts to new inputs, which allows it to make its forecasts. The number of neurons in the hidden layer and the number of hidden layers are determined through experimentation.

OUTPUT LAYER

The output layer is where a neural network's forecasts are made. Two types of real number outputs in financial analysis include forecasts of prices, such as the next day's high and low, and forecasts of technical indicators, such as a predicted moving average value for two days in the future or the next day's stochastic value. Decisions must be made about not only what output to forecast, but also how far into the future to make the forecast.

THE LEARNING PROCESS

Many different learning algorithms can be used to train a neural network, with each algorithm having different performance characteristics. All of the algorithms attempt to minimize the overall error in the network's forecasts.

One popular learning algorithm is the gradient-descent algorithm. However, gradient-descent trains slowly and often finds sub-optimal solutions. This limitation is similar to pitfalls encountered with back-testing and optimization of rule-based trading strategies in which suboptimal sets of parameter values are found that are isolated and unstable.

Training a neural network involves a repetitive mathematical process in which the neural network learns underlying hidden patterns, discerns leads and lags, and identifies nonlinear relationships within the data from repeated exposures to the input data. Learned information is stored by the network in the form of a weight matrix, with changes in the weights occurring as the network "learns."

Similar to the learning process of the human brain, a neural network learns patterns by being exposed to repeated examples of them. Then the neural network generalizes through the learning process to related but previously unseen patterns.

One popular network paradigm that has been used for financial market analysis and forecasting is known as a "feed-forward" network that trains through "back-propagation of error." Once trained, a neural network acts as a market forecasting tool, allowing traders to achieve the trend identification and forecasting goals of technical analysis.

TAILORED FOR EACH MARKET

I have developed intermarket analysis software utilizing the pattern recognition capabilities of neural networks. The program is tailored to each particular target market and uses a series of neural networks, in a two-level hierarchy, to make independent forecasts for a number of different leading technical indicators for that market. The forecasts include tomorrow's predicted high and predicted low, moving averages for short-term, medium-term, and long-term periods, and other leading indicators such as stochastics, MACD, and RSI for the next day.

In addition, another network uses the predictions from those networks as inputs, along with data from the target market and selected related markets, to produce additional proprietary indicators including one called the Neural Index. A Neural Index value of 1.00 indicates that prices are likely to move higher over the next few days, while a value of 0.00 indicates that the market is expected to move lower over the next few days. This indicator is highly accurate at predicting the trend direction in advance.

Although the underlying mathematics of neural network processes is quite complex, the forecasted information is easy for traders to understand, even if they have no background in mathematics and are not experts in technical analysis. You only need to make a quick scan of rising or falling indicator lines or ascending or descending series of indicator values to glean important clues about the expected market direction for each target market.

CAUTION: DON'T OVERTRAIN

In their zeal to get the best results, researchers need to avoid overtraining a neural network. Overtraining occurs when a neural network memorizes the subtleties and idiosyncrasies particular to specific training data without developing the capacity to generalize to new data. Overtraining is analogous to curve-fitting or over-optimization when back-testing and optimizing rule-based trading strategies. An overtrained network will perform poorly on out-of-sample test data and subsequently when making its forecasts during actual trading.

That is why researchers need to evaluate their findings by creating an independent test file made up of data that has not been seen by the neural network during the training process. The neural network is given these new inputs during the testing mode and utilizes the representation that it had previously learned to generate its forecasts. This process, analogous to "walk-forward" or "out-of-sample" testing of rule-based trading systems, allows the network to be evaluated under simulated trading conditions.

> **Trend forecasting strategies based on leading indicators that can anticipate market action offer a substantial competitive advantage.**

Performance results from various neural networks on test data can be compared prior to determining which specific neural network configuration to select for use in the final application. Depending on the comparative test performance results, changes often need to be made in the selection of input data, preprocessing, network architecture, etc., and retraining is usually necessary before the final application network is selected.

With powerful mathematical tools such as neural networks that find patterns and relationships within intermarket data from related global markets, popular technical indicators such as moving averages and MACD can be transformed from single-market lagging indicators into intermarket-based leading indicators.

Because identifying the trend direction is so critical to successful trading, trend forecasting strategies based on leading indicators that can anticipate market action offer a substantial competitive advantage over commonly used trend-following strategies that lag behind market action. The good news is that all you really need to tilt the odds in your favor are reasonably consistent and accurate short-term forecasts regarding the future trend direction of any given target market.

This will give you added confidence and self-discipline to stick with your trading strategies. You'll be able to pull the trigger at the right time without self-doubt or hesitation when there is a strong indication that a market is about to make a top or bottom and is poised to change trend direction. We'll show you how that can be done in the next two chapters.

Chapter 7

USING INTERMARKET DATA FOR PREDICTIVE INDICATORS

The previous chapters made several assertions that most traders should have no difficulty accepting:

- Today's markets are global in nature and highly interconnected.

- Markets influence each other, sometimes in ways not recognizable on the surface.

- Neural networks can be used to find hidden patterns in data and quantify intermarket relationships.

- Most traders still use traditional single-market chart pattern analysis or rely on technical indicators based on past prices from individual markets.

- Most individual traders lose money.

- Mathematically, moving averages and other similarly popular indicators filter out the random "noise" in market data by smoothing out fluctuations and short-term volatility in price movement.

- Because moving averages and other similarly constructed indicators are based on prices that have already occurred in the past, they have an inherent lagging nature, which continues to be a very serious shortcoming and a source of frustration for technical analysts and traders.

- If this deficiency could be overcome somehow, moving averages and other technical indicators that have similar trend-following characteristics would be more effective at trend identification and market forecasting.

- There will never be 100% accuracy when it comes to forecasting market direction or prices for even one or two days in advance. Through financial forecasting, however, mathematical probabilities or expectations of future market action can be used to enhance the performance of trading strategies.

For those traders who recognize the importance of doing something different than what the masses are doing, the value of intermarket analysis and market forecasting made possible by the use of neural networks will become more readily apparent as those tools are applied to the actual trading process.

THE ROAD TO RELIABILITY

The road to a more reliable forecasting process begins with a comprehensive set of price data available through intermarket analysis. Traditional technical indicators are computed using only past price data from a single market so any turning points they indicate will always lag behind the actual turning points in that market. By comparison, a predicted 5-day moving average for two days in the future (based on both single-market and intermarket data) includes the most recent three days' actual prices (which are already known), plus the next two days' prices (which have not yet occurred).

By definition, this predicted moving average would have no lag and would be 100% accurate, if the prices for the next two trading days were somehow known in advance. That's not possible, but if the prediction of the moving average is reasonably accurate, this information can give you a serious competitive advantage over other traders who are only looking backward at past price data, not forward in time.

I have found that predicted moving averages are most effective for trend forecasting when they are produced by analyzing intermarket data and are incorporated into more complex predictive indicators, such as moving average crossover strategies. These strategies can be used to identify not only the anticipated direction of the trend but also its strength. This is accomplished by comparing several predicted moving averages for specific time periods in the future with each other or with today's actual moving averages.

We'll get into several strategies that can be used to capitalize on intermarket analysis in the next chapter, but first we need to look at the types of predictive technical indicators that can be created by applying neural networks to intermarket data. To illustrate the kind of predictive information that can be derived through this analytical approach, we'll explore in more detail some of the capabilities and predictive information provided by the current version of VantagePoint Intermarket Analysis Software. This software applies the pattern recognition capabilities of neural networks in order to analyze internal market data from each target market and external intermarket data from 25 closely related intermarkets to make forecasts for the target market.

VantagePoint's various charted forecasts and predicted technical indicators can be displayed on its Daily Report, History Report, or on VantagePoint charts. (The acronyms in parenthesis show how the indicators are identified in the status bars on VantagePoint charts.)

PREDICTED NEURAL INDEX

The Predicted Neural Index (PIndex) is a proprietary indicator that predicts whether or not a 3-day simple moving average of the typical price (the average of the high, low, and close prices for the day) will be higher or lower two days in the future than it is today. The Neural Index compares two 3-day moving averages to one another—today's actual 3-day moving average with a predicted 3-day moving average. The forecast of the predicted 3-day moving average is made by a neural network, using predictions from four other networks as inputs, in addition to data from the target market itself and the 25 related markets pertaining to that target market.

When the predicted 3-day moving average value is greater than today's actual 3-day moving average value, the Neural Index is "1.00," indicating that the market is expected to move higher over the next two days. When the predicted 3-day moving average value is less than today's actual 3-day moving average value, the Neural Index is "0.00," indicating the market is expected to move lower over the next two days. Review the information in Figures 7.1 and 7.2.

The Neural Index will always be either correct or incorrect, so its performance can be measured precisely in terms of percent correct. The Neural Index is the source of the accuracy statistics cited for VantagePoint, which has a predictive accuracy rate of around 80% across a wide range of markets and time spans in ongoing research.

With a high accuracy rate, the Neural Index gives traders added confidence to pull the trigger when used in conjunction with other indicators showing a strong indication that a market is about to make a top or bottom and is poised to change trend direction.

FIGURE 7.1 - THE DAILY REPORT

ACTUAL MARKET DATA

Open	High	Low	Close
656.1	658.7	647.4	650.6
651.5	658.0	646.7	654.8
657.6	666.0	655.3	662.5
662.1	667.0	660.3	664.4
665.0	667.8	661.3	662.1
661.9	671.0	661.8	668.3
668.0	669.9	664.4	667.3

VANTAGEPOINT FORECASTS

Predicted Neural Index	Predicted Next Day High	Predicted Next Day Low	Predicted Short Term Difference	Predicted Medium Term Difference	Predicted Long Term Difference
0.00	655.6	646.9	-0.7	1.0	-0.9
1.00	659.4	651.4	0.2	2.1	-0.1
1.00	667.8	659.7	3.8	5.5	2.4
1.00	670.8	656.5	5.2	6.6	3.9
1.00	668.5	657.7	3.9	5.7	5.2
1.00	673.6	665.5	4.6	6.9	7.6
1.00	672.8	664.5	2.9	6.8	8.3

Shows Actual Price Data, Forecasted data and the Neural Index

*Note the shift from 0.00 to 1.00 on July 6 (underlined) on the table in the forecast section, a confirmation of underlying strength for a long position.

VANTAGEPOINT INTERMARKET ANALYSIS SOFTWARE

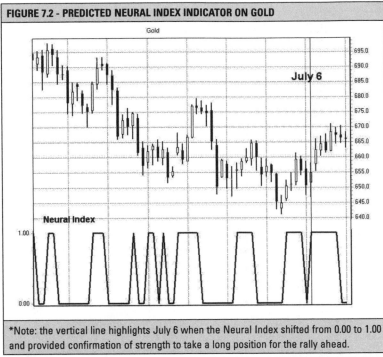

FIGURE 7.2 - PREDICTED NEURAL INDEX INDICATOR ON GOLD

*Note: the vertical line highlights July 6 when the Neural Index shifted from 0.00 to 1.00 and provided confirmation of strength to take a long position for the rally ahead.

VANTAGEPOINT INTERMARKET ANALYSIS SOFTWARE

PREDICTED STRENGTH

Predicted Strength (PStr) is a 3-day moving average predicted two days ahead minus the current 3-day moving average. Predicted Strength is a confirming indicator that can help you identify the market showing the most strength or weakness. It also indicates if the market is getting overbought or oversold. If the predictive indicators in a number of markets suggest trading opportunities, the Predicted Strength can help you determine which market offers the best potential.

A value close to zero means that there will be little difference between the predicted and current moving averages. A relatively high Predicted Strength value indicates that the predicted moving average

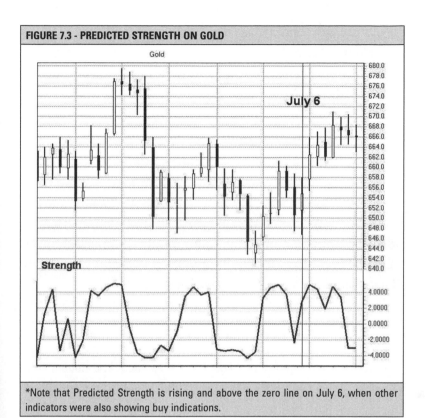

FIGURE 7.3 - PREDICTED STRENGTH ON GOLD

*Note that Predicted Strength is rising and above the zero line on July 6, when other indicators were also showing buy indications.

VANTAGEPOINT INTERMARKET ANALYSIS SOFTWARE

will be much higher than the current moving average. (See Figure 7.3) A relatively low Predicted Strength value indicates that the predicted moving average will be much lower than the current moving average. Predicted Strength numbers vary from market to market; there are no maximum or minimum Predicted Strength values.

PREDICTED MOVING AVERAGES

The purpose of moving averages is to smooth out the daily fluctuations in price so the underlying trend can be observed. Unfortunately, moving averages introduce lag time. Take the following hypothetical example of a rising price:

Monday $1

Tuesday $2

Wednesday $3

Thursday $4

Friday $5

On Friday, the price is $5, but a 5-day simple moving average of the price would be (1 + 2 + 3 + 4 + 5) / 5 = $3. In this example, a 5-day simple moving average introduced two days of lag. If the price for next Monday and Tuesday were known on Friday:

Next Monday $6

Next Tuesday $7

Then a predicted 5-day simple moving average could be calculated as (3 + 4 + 5 + 6 + 7) / 5 = $5. Thus, we get the benefit of smoothing with low lag. The idea behind VantagePoint is to use neural networks and intermarket analysis to produce low-lag, predicted moving averages. (See Figure 7.4)

Using "typical prices" (the average of the day's high, low, and close prices) as the data source, VantagePoint presents predicted exponential moving averages (EMA) for six time periods and simple moving averages (SMA) of the close for three time periods for use with a series of predicted indicators:

- Predicted 2-day EMA Typical One Day
  Ahead (P2EMA+1)

- Predicted 3-day EMA Typical One Day Ahead (P3EMA+1)

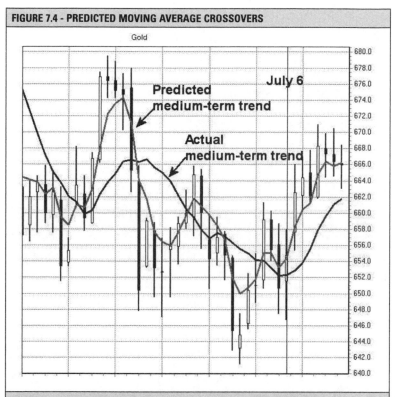

FIGURE 7.4 - PREDICTED MOVING AVERAGE CROSSOVERS

*Note that the predicted moving average (gray line) often turns several days before the actual moving average (black line). How you trade these indications depends on how aggressive you want to be as a trader.

VANTAGEPOINT INTERMARKET ANALYSIS SOFTWARE

- Predicted 4-day EMA Typical Two Days Ahead (P4EMA+2)

- Predicted 6-day EMA Typical Three Days Ahead (P6EMA+3)

- Predicted 8-day EMA Typical Two Days Ahead (P8EMA+2)

- Predicted 18-day EMA Typical Three Days Ahead
  (P18EMA+3)

- Actual 5-day SMA close (A5SMA)

- Actual 10-day SMA close (A10SMA)

- Actual 15-day SMA close (A15SMA)

PREDICTED CROSSOVERS

VantagePoint presents crossover indicators in four pre-defined chart formats. In general, when VantagePoint's predicted moving average crosses above (or below) the actual moving average, VantagePoint expects the market trend to turn up (or down) within the forecast time horizon related to each of these indicators.

The crossover indicators are not predicting the trend several days in the future but are using the price predicted several days in the future to reduce the lag in the trend normally associated with moving averages.

- **Predicted Short Term Crossover**—the Predicted 2-day Exponential Moving Average of Typical Prices One Day Ahead (P2EMA+1) crosses above or below the Actual 5-day Simple Moving Average of the Close (A5SMA).

- **Predicted Medium Term Crossover**—the Predicted 4-day Exponential Moving Average of Typical Prices Two Days Ahead (P4EMA+2) crosses above or below the Actual 10-day Simple Moving Average of the Close (A10SMA).

- **Predicted Long Term Crossover**—the Predicted 6-day Exponential Moving Average of Typical Prices Three Days

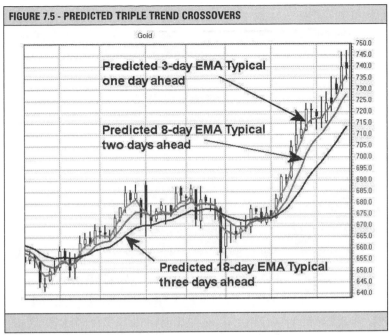

FIGURE 7.5 - PREDICTED TRIPLE TREND CROSSOVERS

VANTAGEPOINT INTERMARKET ANALYSIS SOFTWARE

Ahead (P6EMA+3) crosses above or below the Actual
15-day Simple Moving Average of the Close (A15SMA).

VantagePoint also presents a pre-defined **Predicted Triple Crossover**
indicator, which predicts a change in market trend direction when the
Predicted 3-day EMA Typical One Day Ahead crosses the Predicted
8-day EMA Typical Two Days Ahead, and this prediction is confirmed
when the Predicted 8-day EMA Typical Two Days Ahead crosses the
Predicted 18-day EMA Typical Three Days Ahead. (See Figure 7.5)

Traders can use the default settings for these crossover indicators or
can create their own Triple Crossover or other custom charts that con-
tain any or all of these predictive indicators. Choosing among short-
term, medium-term, and long-term crossovers requires balancing lag

time against false crossovers. The short-term crossovers have the least amount of lag but the most false crossovers. Conversely, the long-term crossovers occur a day or two later but avoid most false crossovers. The idea is to screen out the daily fluctuations so you can observe the underlying trend with as little lag as possible.

PREDICTED DIFFERENCES

In addition to looking at a chart to spot the crossover indicators visually, VantagePoint also compares the exponential and actual moving averages against each other to produce another set of indicators based on the differences between the moving averages. These differences will forecast strengthening or weakening market trends.

- **Predicted Short Term Difference (PTSDiff)**—the amount the Predicted 2-day EMA Typical One Day Ahead (P2EMA+1) is above or below the Actual 5-day SMA of the Close (A5SMA).

- **Predicted Medium Term Difference (PTMDiff)**—the amount the Predicted 4-day EMA Typical Two Days Ahead (P4EMA+2) is above or below the Actual 10-day SMA of the Close (A10SMA).

- **Predicted Long Term Difference (PTLDiff)**—the amount the Predicted 6-day EMA Typical Three Days Ahead (P6EMA+3) is above or below the Actual 15-day SMA of the Close (A15SMA).

As VantagePoint's neural networks are updated each day with the most recent data on the target market and its 25 related markets, VantagePoint makes its forecasts and calculates the difference in value between each predicted moving average and the actual moving aver-

FIGURE 7.6 - DAILY REPORT SHOWING PREDICTED DIFFERENCES

ACTUAL MARKET DATA

Open	High	Low	Close
656.1	658.7	647.4	650.6
651.5	658.0	646.7	654.8
657.6	666.0	655.3	662.5
662.1	667.0	660.3	664.4
665.0	667.8	661.3	662.1
661.9	671.0	661.8	668.3
668.0	669.9	664.4	667.3

VANTAGEPOINT FORECASTS

Predicted Neural Index	Predicted Next Day High	Predicted Next Day Low	Predicted Short Term Difference	Predicted Medium Term Difference	Predicted Long Term Difference
0.00	655.6	646.9	-0.7	1.0	-0.9
1.00	659.4	651.4	0.2	2.1	-0.1
1.00	667.8	659.7	3.8	5.5	2.4
1.00	670.8	656.5	5.2	6.6	3.9
1.00	668.5	657.7	3.9	5.7	5.2
1.00	673.6	665.5	4.6	6.9	7.6
1.00	672.8	664.5	2.9	6.8	8.3

* Note the larger numbers on July 6 (underlined) compared to July 5 (day before) for the short-term and medium-term difference and the smaller negative number for the long-term difference, supporting the Neural Index indication for a long position.

VANTAGEPOINT INTERMARKET ANALYSIS SOFTWARE

age. By using forecasted moving averages, VantagePoint retains all of the smoothing effects of moving averages while effectively eliminating their lag.

VantagePoint offers several choices for displaying the difference data. If you prefer to look at numerical values, the Daily Report (Figure 7.6) provides the predicted difference indicator values in three columns related to the time frame of your trading strategy. If a series of differ-

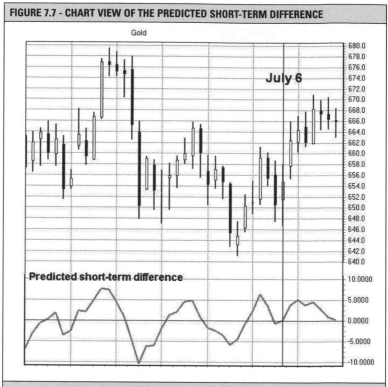

FIGURE 7.7 - CHART VIEW OF THE PREDICTED SHORT-TERM DIFFERENCE

Gold

July 6

Predicted short-term difference

*Note that the angle of the line has turned up on July 6 (vertical line) when the Neural Index has moved from 0.00 to 1.00, indicating a bullish condition.

VANTAGEPOINT INTERMARKET ANALYSIS SOFTWARE

ence numbers changes from negative to positive or the numbers become less negative, it suggests strength and the market trend may rise. If a series of difference numbers changes from positive to negative or the numbers become less positive, it suggests weakness and the market trend may decline.

If you prefer a more visual display, the difference values can be shown on the bottom of a VantagePoint chart. (See Figure 7.7) If the chart shows a predicted moving average crossover, the slope or angle of the predicted

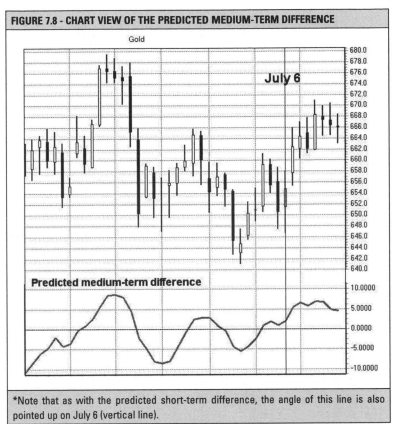

FIGURE 7.8 - CHART VIEW OF THE PREDICTED MEDIUM-TERM DIFFERENCE

*Note that as with the predicted short-term difference, the angle of this line is also pointed up on July 6 (vertical line).

VANTAGEPOINT INTERMARKET ANALYSIS SOFTWARE

difference indicator(s) should be in agreement with the slope or angle of the predicted moving average to provide confirmation for a trade.

BEATING THE LAG

When the PTSDiff is positive, reaches a maximum positive value, and begins to narrow (indicating that the upward trend is beginning to lose strength), you gain an early warning that the market is about to make a top and turn down within the next day.

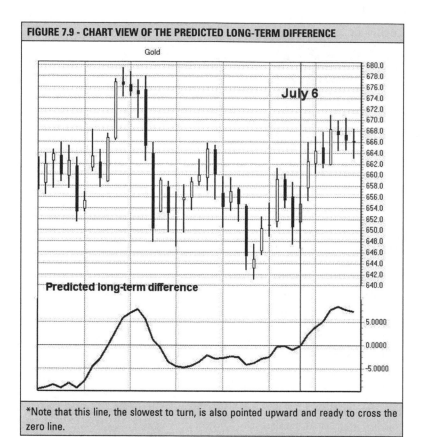

FIGURE 7.9 - CHART VIEW OF THE PREDICTED LONG-TERM DIFFERENCE

Gold

July 6

Predicted long-term difference

*Note that this line, the slowest to turn, is also pointed upward and ready to cross the zero line.

VANTAGEPOINT INTERMARKET ANALYSIS SOFTWARE

When the PTMDiff is positive, reaches a maximum positive value, and begins to narrow (indicating that the upward trend is beginning to lose strength), this provides an early warning that the market is about to make a top and turn down within the next two days. (See Figure 7.8)

When the PTLDiff is positive, reaches a maximum positive value, and begins to narrow (indicating that the upward trend is beginning to lose strength), this provides an early warning that the market is about to make a top and turn down within the next three days. (See Figure 7.9)

FIGURE 7.10 - DAILY REPORT SHOWING PREDICTED DIFFERENCES

ACTUAL MARKET DATA

Open	High	Low	Close
656.1	658.7	647.4	650.6
651.5	658.0	646.7	654.8
657.6	666.0	655.3	662.5
662.1	667.0	660.3	664.4
665.0	667.8	661.3	662.1
661.9	671.0	661.8	668.3
668.0	669.9	664.4	667.3

VANTAGEPOINT FORECASTS

Predicted Neural Index	Predicted Next Day High	Predicted Next Day Low	Predicted Short Term Difference	Predicted Medium Term Difference	Predicted Long Term Difference
0.00	655.6	646.9	-0.7	1.0	-0.9
1.00	659.4	651.4	0.2	2.1	-0.1
1.00	667.8	659.7	3.8	5.5	2.4
1.00	670.8	656.5	5.2	6.6	3.9
1.00	668.5	657.7	3.9	5.7	5.2
1.00	673.6	665.5	4.6	6.9	7.6
1.00	672.8	664.5	2.9	6.8	8.3

Even though the predicted long-term difference was higher than the day before and the Neural Index was still at 1.00 on the Daily Report after trading on July 11 (underlined), you might have wanted to exit a long position or placed a sell stop because the numbers for predicted short-term and predicted medium-term differences were smaller, assuming this might be an early alert for a market change.

VANTAGEPOINT INTERMARKET ANALYSIS SOFTWARE

When the PTSDiff is negative, reaches a maximum negative value, and begins to narrow (indicating that the downward trend is beginning to lose strength), you are seeing an early warning that the market is about to make a bottom and turn up within the next day.

When the PTMDiff is negative, reaches a maximum negative value, and starts to narrow (indicating that the downward trend is beginning

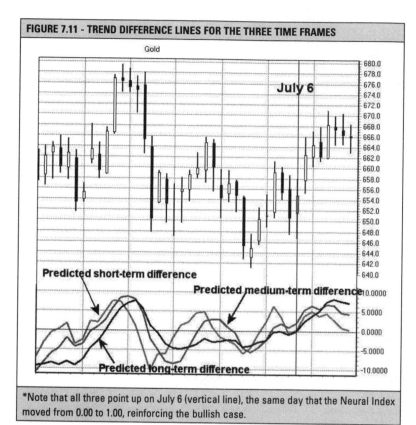

FIGURE 7.11 - TREND DIFFERENCE LINES FOR THE THREE TIME FRAMES

Gold

July 6

Predicted short-term difference

Predicted medium-term difference

Predicted long-term difference

*Note that all three point up on July 6 (vertical line), the same day that the Neural Index moved from 0.00 to 1.00, reinforcing the bullish case.

VANTAGEPOINT INTERMARKET ANALYSIS SOFTWARE

to lose strength), this provides an early warning that the market is about to make a bottom and turn up within the next two days.

When the PTLDiff is negative, reaches a maximum negative value, and begins to narrow (indicating that the downward trend is beginning to lose strength), this provides an early warning that the market is about to make a bottom and turn up within the next three days.

EARLY WARNING ACTIONS

Predicted difference indicators can be used in conjunction with the Predicted Neural Index to confirm the trend direction or to indicate that a trend may be ready to reverse. Note how the predicted difference numbers on the Daily Report (Figure 7.10) relate to the Predicted Neural Index reading for the same day. How aggressively you wish to trade the changes in numbers or the slope of the indicator will depend on your trading strategy and risk propensity.

Figure 7.11 provides a composite view of the predicted differences for the three time frames on a VantagePoint chart. Note that the slope of the predicted difference and the related moving average should both point upward and the Predicted Neural Index should be at 1.00 to confirm strength that will cause the market trend to rise. Similarly, if the difference numbers change from positive to negative or become less positive, if the slope of the predicted difference and related moving averages both point downward, and if the Predicted Neural Index is 0.00, it suggests weakness and the market trend may decline.

Rather than wait for the crossover on the chart to actually occur, aggressive traders can make trading decisions based on the initial narrowing in the PTSDiff, PTMDiff, or PTLDiff, which gives the earliest warning that the market trend is beginning to lose strength. You can act on this information in a number of ways, depending on your account size, risk propensity, information derived from single-market technical indicators, and/or other criteria. For instance, if you are in a long position, here are just three possible ways to capitalize on these early alerts:

If the PTSDiff, PTMDiff, or PTLDiff reach a maximum positive value and narrow by even a small amount, you can close out your long position and stand aside. Then you can wait for the numbers to either narrow further or for one, two, or all three of them to turn negative before taking a short trade, even if the Neural Index has still not changed to 0.00. If the PTSDiff, PTMDiff, or PTLDiff (or all of them) begin to show renewed strength instead (the difference between the predicted and the actual moving average value widens again instead of continues to narrow), you could re-enter your long position.

If the PTSDiff, PTMDiff, or PTLDiff reach a maximum positive value and narrow by even a small amount and the Neural Index is 1.00, you could tighten your stop and stay in your long position. That keeps you in a long position should the market show renewed strength. If, instead, the difference continues to narrow on subsequent days, you would close out your long position and stand aside or reverse positions.

If the PTSDiff, PTMDiff, or PTLDiff reach a maximum positive value and narrow by a predetermined minimum amount, you can close out your long position and go short, even if the Neural Index has still not changed to 0.00. This is the most aggressive approach of the three because it involves reversing positions at the earliest indication that the current market trend is likely to make a top and change direction.

Likewise, if you are short, you would wait for the PTSDiff, PTMDiff, or PTLDiff to reach a maximum negative value and narrow before following any of these three strategies.

To the extent that the PTSDiff, PTMDiff, and PTLDiff behave similarly to each other from one day to the next (and are confirmed by the Neural Index), you can be more confident that the market will move as expected within the forecast time horizons of these indicators. This can also be useful in determining stop placement. (See Figure 7.12) By creating trend forecasting strategies, which compare predicted moving averages with actual moving averages, you can get an early warning

FIGURE 7.12 - PROTECTIVE STOP PLACEMENT

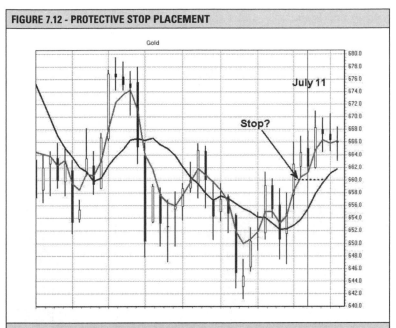

*The chart illustrates where you might have placed a protective sell stop below the lows on a long position when the predicted short-term and predicted medium-term difference numbers were smaller on July 11 (vertical line) than the day before. In this case, the stop would not have been hit and you would still have been able to benefit from the price runup on July 12.

of an impending change in trend direction, sometimes days before it would show up on a traditional price chart or be identified by single-market, trend-following indicators such as popular moving average crossover approaches.

PREDICTED NEXT DAY HIGHS AND LOWS

Based on actual and predicted prices, VantagePoint also produces forecasts for the next day's expected high and low. (See Figure 7.13) Knowing the probabilities for the next day's range, day traders can

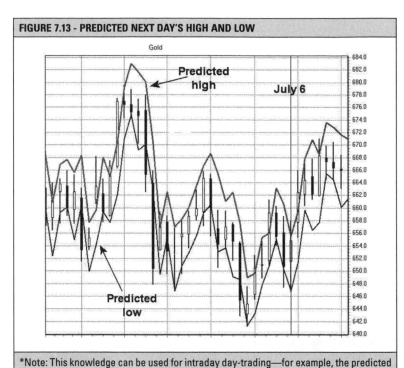

FIGURE 7.13 - PREDICTED NEXT DAY'S HIGH AND LOW

Gold

Predicted high

July 6

Predicted low

*Note: This knowledge can be used for intraday day-trading—for example, the predicted low for July 6 (vertical line) was 646.9 and the actual low was 646.7—or for placement of stops (see Chapter 8).

VANTAGEPOINT INTERMARKET ANALYSIS SOFTWARE

position themselves within these targets, or position traders can use breakouts of the predicted range to take positions or to place stops.

PREDICTED NEXT DAY HIGH (PHIGH)

This indicator predicts the high price for the next day. On Figure 7.13, the values of the next day's predicted highs and lows are displaced one trading day into the future; so, the predicted highs and lows are charted on the day for which the values are expected to occur, much like a chart showing a displaced moving average. On the Daily Report (Figure 7.14), the next day's predicted highs and lows are shown on the day the predictions were made.

FIGURE 7.14 - DAILY REPORT SHOWING PREDICTED NEXT DAY'S HIGH AND LOW

ACTUAL MARKET DATA

Open	High	Low	Close
656.1	658.7	647.4	650.6
651.5	658.0	646.7	654.8
657.6	666.0	655.3	662.5
662.1	667.0	660.3	664.4
665.0	667.8	661.3	662.1
661.9	671.0	661.8	668.3
668.0	669.9	664.4	667.3

VANTAGEPOINT FORECASTS

Predicted Neural Index	Predicted Next Day High	Predicted Next Day Low	Predicted Short Term Difference	Predicted Medium Term Difference	Predicted Long Term Difference
0.00	655.6	646.9	-0.7	1.0	-0.9
1.00	659.4	651.4	0.2	2.1	-0.1
1.00	667.8	659.7	3.8	5.5	2.4
1.00	670.8	656.5	5.2	6.6	3.9
1.00	668.5	657.7	3.9	5.7	5.2
1.00	673.6	665.5	4.6	6.9	7.6
1.00	672.8	664.5	2.9	6.8	8.3

*Note: The predicted low for July 6 (underlined) of 646.9 shows up on the July 5 line, the day the forecast was made.

VANTAGEPOINT INTERMARKET ANALYSIS SOFTWARE

PREDICTED NEXT DAY LOW (PLOW)

Like the predicted next day high, this indicator predicts the low price for the next day. Taken together, the values for the predicted next day high and predicted next day low create a predicted trading range for the next day. Knowing the probabilities for the next day's trading range helps traders to pinpoint values for intraday entry and exit points or to determine breakouts of the expected range to help determine where to place stops, as discussed in the next chapter.

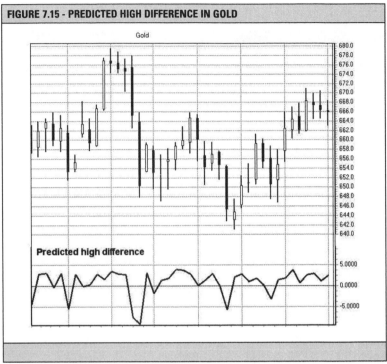

FIGURE 7.15 - PREDICTED HIGH DIFFERENCE IN GOLD

VANTAGEPOINT INTERMARKET ANALYSIS SOFTWARE

PREDICTED HIGH DIFFERENCE

This is the difference between the predicted high and the actual high price for the day. These readings can help you assess the strength or weakness of a trend. (See Figure 7.15)

PREDICTED LOW DIFFERENCE

This is the difference between the predicted low and the actual low price for the day. These readings can help you assess the strength or weakness of a trend. (See Figure 7.16)

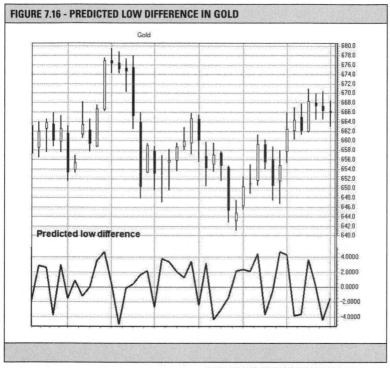

FIGURE 7.16 - PREDICTED LOW DIFFERENCE IN GOLD

PREDICTED MOMENTUM INDICATORS

VantagePoint displays several predicted momentum indicators using data provided by intermarket analysis as the price input. Momentum indicators in general can be used in several ways:

- **Value and position of the indicator line itself—** the location of the indicator reading on a scale typically between 0 and 100 reflects when a price trend may be weakening or strengthening by comparing the current value with previous values.

- **Overbought/oversold**—if the predicted momentum indicator exceeds a prescribed boundary, this indicates the market may be becoming overbought or oversold. The market may be due for a correction that will bring the indicator value back within the specified range.

- **Divergence**—divergence between the predicted momentum indicator and market prices may indicate imminent changes in market sentiment. For example, if prices are still falling and make a lower low but the predicted momentum indicator turns upward and makes higher lows, this could indicate a bullish turn. If the predicted momentum indicator turns downward and makes lower highs while prices are still rising and reaching new highs, this could indicate a bearish turn.

Momentum indicators work best when a market is in choppy conditions and is trading within a range that is sufficiently wide enough to provide trading opportunities between the high and low prices. When a market moves into an extended trend, momentum indicators may give false information for long periods of time before the price trend actually does change.

Momentum indicators are usually displayed below the price bars or candlesticks on a chart. However, VantagePoint predicted momentum indicators are shown alone on a chart in the following examples so you can see them in more detail.

PREDICTED MACD (PMACD)

VantagePoint predicts the Moving Average Convergence Divergence (MACD) indicator one day ahead. MACD is a familiar trend-following momentum indicator using moving averages. Predicted MACD charts

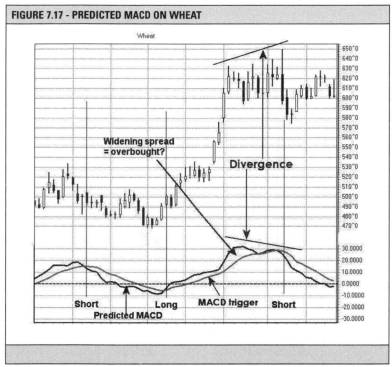

FIGURE 7.17 - PREDICTED MACD ON WHEAT

VANTAGEPOINT INTERMARKET ANALYSIS SOFTWARE

the difference between a longer-term predicted exponential moving average (26-day) and a shorter-term predicted exponential moving average (12-day). The **MACD Trigger** is calculated as a 9-day exponential moving average of the MACD predicted one day ahead.

MACD can be used as a crossover indicator when the Predicted MACD crosses above or below the Trigger line or the zero line; or as an overbought/oversold indicator when the Predicted MACD pulls away from the Trigger; or as a divergence indicator when the Predicted MACD is moving in one direction and the market price is moving in the opposite direction, suggesting an upcoming change in market sentiment before it becomes evident on a price chart (as shown on Figure 7.17).

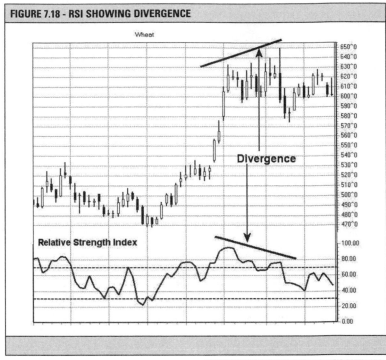

FIGURE 7.18 - RSI SHOWING DIVERGENCE

VANTAGEPOINT INTERMARKET ANALYSIS SOFTWARE

PREDICTED RSI (PRSI)

This momentum indicator predicts the 14-day Relative Strength Index (RSI) one day ahead. (See Figure 7.18) RSI compares an average of *up* closes to an average of *down* closes for the previous 14 days to predict a market's strength or weakness and is plotted on a scale of 0 to 100. Readings above 70 indicate an overbought market; readings below 30 indicate an oversold situation. Predictions above 70 or below 30 suggest that the market may be making a top or bottom in the next day.

With thresholds of 30 and 70, RSI measures the strength of market moves and provides some timely warnings. However, like some other momentum indicators, it does not do well in trending conditions and

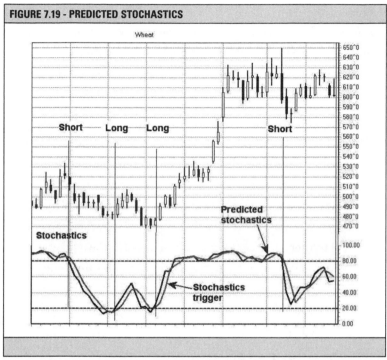

FIGURE 7.19 - PREDICTED STOCHASTICS

needs to be used in conjunction with other indicators. Like other indicators, divergence is a clue to a potential trend change.

PREDICTED STOCHASTIC (PSTOCH)

This is an example of a momentum indicator that compares a market's closing price to its price range over a period of time and indicates when a price trend may be weakening or strengthening. (See Figure 7.19) Predicted Stochastic forecasts a 14-day stochastic oscillator (%K) one day ahead. The **Stochastic Trigger** predicts a three-day moving average (%D) of the stochastic oscillator one day ahead.

The Predicted Stochastic indicator is based on the position of the close relative to the high or low of the day. During periods of price decreases, the daily closes tend to accumulate near the daily lows. During periods of price increases, the daily closes tend to accumulate near the daily highs. The Predicted Stochastic indicator is an oscillator that is designed to predict overbought and oversold conditions one day in advance.

The Predicted Stochastic charts two lines: Predicted Stochastic (%K) and Stochastic Trigger (%D), which are plotted on a scale ranging from 0 to 100. Readings above 80 predict an overbought condition; readings below 20 predict an oversold condition. The Predicted Stochastic line (%K) is faster and more sensitive than the Stochastic Trigger line (%D). When %K crosses over the %D line in overbought (>80) or oversold (<20) territory, this could be an indication that the market is about to reverse direction. Predicted Stochastics provides timely moves in choppy conditions, dropping down from above 80 and moving up from below 20. But like some other indicators, it doesn't fare so well when the market trends higher.

PREDICTED TRUE STRENGTH INDEX (PTSI)

The Predicted True Strength Index predicts the True Strength Index (TSI) one day ahead. (See Figure 7.20) It is known as a "double smoothed" moving average because a 20-day exponential moving average is applied to the difference in predicted typical prices and then a 10-day EMA is applied to the result. **TSI Trigger (Trigger)** is a 7-day exponential moving average of the Predicted TSI. Trend and momentum changes are predicted when the PTSI line crosses the trigger line.

The TSI is another momentum indicator that can help to determine if a market is overbought or oversold. Values range between +100 and -100, and the default overbought and oversold levels are set to +25 and -25. This is another momentum indicator that fares better in choppy conditions than it does in trending conditions.

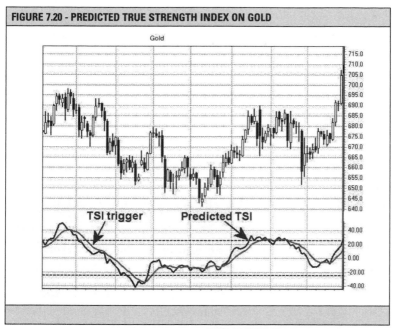

FIGURE 7.20 - PREDICTED TRUE STRENGTH INDEX ON GOLD

VANTAGEPOINT INTERMARKET ANALYSIS SOFTWARE

PUTTING PREDICTIVE INDICATORS TO WORK

Using intermarket analysis in conjunction with neural networks, VantagePoint provides a wealth of predictive indicators that can give you a trading edge over other traders who are still relying solely on single-market, lagging indicators. Unlike traditional charts, when the predictive indicators are displayed on a chart, you see where the market is expected to go next, not just where it has been in the past. Although many traders still rely on single-market, trend-following indicators that look backward and can only identify trend changes after the fact, predictive indicators give you a roadmap that looks forward to give you a sneak preview of what lies ahead.

These predictive indicators can be used in conjunction with each other or with techniques you are already using to develop more robust trading strategies. For example, you can use the PTSDiff and the PTMDiff indicators with the Neural Index to confirm the expected market direction. The strongest confirmation occurs when the Neural Index, PTSDiff, and PTMDiff are in agreement with each other.

VantagePoint's neural networks are updated each trading day with the most recent data on the target market and its 25 related markets. Its forecasted moving averages retain all of the smoothing effects of moving averages while effectively eliminating the lag. By creating trend forecasting strategies (comparing predicted moving averages with actual moving averages is just one example of what VantagePoint offers you in the way of predictive information), you can get an early warning of an impending change in trend direction, often days before it would show up on a traditional price chart or before it would be identified by single-market, trend-following indicators.

PLAYING THE ODDS

Unfortunately, you will never be able to forecast market direction or prices in advance with 100% predictive accuracy. Financial forecasting, nevertheless, can help you formulate mathematical expectations and probabilities of what is likely to happen in the future. Needless to say, the further out the time horizon, the less reliable the forecast. But a lead time of even just one day is more than enough to gain a tremendous trading advantage.

Once you have identified the expected trend direction using any of the various predictive indicators that forecast changes in trend direction, you can set your entry and exit points that reflect your risk propensity and meet your trading objectives. To help you do this, you can use the predictive indicators for the next day's predicted high and predicted low. By creating an expected trading range for the next day, these price forecasts are analogous to extending support and resistance lines in traditional single-market technical analysis approaches. Using predicted high and predicted low forecasts based on the pattern recognition capabilities of neural networks applied to intermarket data, you have objectively determined entry, exit, or stop points. In this way, you do not have to rely only on an arbitrary linear extrapolation from past single-market data.

Day traders can use the forecasts of the next day's predicted high and predicted low to identify low-risk day trades; waiting for the market to trade up toward the predicted high on an expected down day before entering a short position, or waiting for the market to trade down toward the predicted low before entering a long position on a day when prices are expected to move up. Position traders can use the forecasts of the next day's predicted high or predicted low to enter positions, and then use the subsequent days' forecasts to move their stop or exit the trade.

One benefit of setting your stops using forecasts of the next day's predicted high or predicted low is that your stops are less likely to be clustered among other traders' stops, which are typically placed at relatively obvious places such as at support and resistance lines.

MULTI-MARKET CONFIRMATION

Because the neural networks have been developed and trained independently for each particular target market, Daily Reports from other target markets can be used for additional confirmation. The Daily Reports for the Eurodollar, 2-year Treasury notes, 5-year Treasury notes, and 30-year Treasury bonds, for example, add considerable insight into what is likely to happen to 10-year Treasury notes because these five markets together encompass the entire interest rate yield curve from 90 days to 30 years.

The more the forecasted indicators on these other reports confirm the indicators on the 10-year Treasury note Daily Report, the higher the probability that the Treasury note market will act as expected. On the other hand, if these other reports give contrary indications, you should be cautious about taking a trade in Treasury notes. Similar confirmations or divergences can be found among the energy markets, stock indexes, currencies, and other markets.

Often, VantagePoint is used by traders as an intermarket confirmation tool in conjunction with other tools that they may already be using. In this way VantagePoint's predictive indicators act as filters to various single-market indicators that only look internally at each market. When VantagePoint confirms these single-market indicators from an intermarket perspective, then it is a green light to take the trade. However, when VantagePoint is in disagreement with these single-market indicators, that's a bright yellow caution light. Other traders have developed successful trading strategies that rely only upon the predictive information provided by VantagePoint.

If you can appreciate the advantage of having intermarket-based trend forecasts predicting short-term market direction with nearly 80% accuracy and the benefit of broadening your perspective of the markets beyond the internal dynamics within each individual market, then you will become a believer in applying intermarket analysis to your trading.

The next chapter will provide a few example strategies that apply some of these predictive indicators to real market situations. This will help you learn how to know when a market is ready to turn and show how you can get onboard the trends. Predictive indicators based on intermarket analysis and neural networks give you a tremendous amount of information to help you make more effective trading decisions.

Chapter 8

APPLYING PREDICTIVE INDICATORS TO TRADING STRATEGIES

Most traders are eager to get some kind of trading edge—the few extra minutes or days spent studying the markets or the added insight from applying some new indicator that increases the odds that their trading will be more successful than it was before. By doing some form of intermarket analysis traders could benefit from predictive indicators to provide market forecasts; this is the edge they are seeking and, more important, desperately need in today's global economy.

Just having access to predictive indicators, however, does not assure trading success. Successful traders still need to develop methods or strategies with which they are comfortable and in which they have complete confidence so that when the markets become volatile (as is frequently the case due to their interconnectedness), traders will have a coherent trading framework on which they can rely.

This chapter will discuss several basic strategies for using predictive indicators produced by VantagePoint Intermarket Analysis Software in conjunction with candlestick analysis and fundamentals—such as the potentially volatile pricing periods associated with U.S. Fed Open Market Committee or other central bank policy meetings, or reports about jobs, company earnings, crops, energy stockpiles, weather, and the like—in a synergistic analytical approach described more fully in the next chapter.

Many VantagePoint users have developed numerous strategies with the software, adding tweaks here and there to suit their style, so it would be impossible to include all of the trading ideas that are possible. With the number and variety of predictive indicators in VantagePoint, strategies are limited only by the trader's imagination. For further analysis of the predictive indicators, VantagePoint data can be exported to an Excel spreadsheet and massaged further, depending on how elaborate you want your strategies to be.

Before delving into the details of the sample strategies, several points need to be emphasized at the onset; otherwise, there is a tendency among traders to develop unrealistic expectations about trading:

- No strategy or indicator can be guaranteed to work 100% of the time. There is no such thing in trading. All you can hope to achieve is an improved probability of success through the use of predictive indicators.

- Predictive indicators—or any indicators, for that matter— should not be used in isolation. Traders should apply predictive indicators in conjunction with traditional chart pattern analysis and market fundamentals in a synergistic trading approach. As with candlestick analysis, the location of an indicator alert within the context of a price move is very important—that is, a buy indication that occurs after an extended downtrend is more likely to be legitimate than a buy indication that occurs after the market has already had an extended rally.

- The comments below cover only the basics of the strategies discussed. There are countless variations to these strategies that can be implemented, and traders should feel free to conduct their own research to expand on or modify these strategies to suit their own trading style and comfort levels.

- VantagePoint is an analytical software tool that provides intermarket-based predictive information. It is not a trading system per se that produces specific buy/sell signals.

- Traders looking for comments on these strategies and others in current market situations or for more ideas about trading should check www.TraderChat.com and www.TraderEducation.com, two websites that many VantagePoint users have found informative.

TRADING STRATEGY PREMISES

Time frames may vary, but trading strategies can be placed into one of two broad categories:

1. **Trading with the breakout.** When a market breaks through some kind of boundary—a trend line, moving average, support or resistance—the assumption is that prices will follow through on the breakout and launch a new trend. Not every breakout leads to a new trend, of course, but strategies based on breakouts and trend-following techniques count on riding longer extended trends following the breakout to more than offset those times when the breakout fails and results in small losses.

2. **Trading against the breakout.** When a market approaches some kind of boundary—a trend line, pivot points,

moving average, support or resistance—the assumption is
that prices will back away from that boundary and not break
through into a new trend. Prices will eventually break through
the boundary, of course, but these revert-to-the-mean-types
of momentum strategies count on the market's tendency to
respect key price points and maintain the trading range that is
in place.

VantagePoint offers predictive indicators that, when used with candlestick analysis and an assessment of where price action is occurring
on a chart, can provide useful information for both types of trading
strategies. In most cases, VantagePoint data can be viewed in either
a tabular format on the Daily Report or History Report or in a more
visual form on a chart, depending on your personal preference. You
need to take some time to work with VantagePoint's predictive indicators to determine which ones suit your style best. All of the indicators
can give added insight into what's happening in a given market, and
therefore can augment the typical single-market, lagging indicators
that you may be using.

Before getting into some strategy examples, the following are some
general observations about VantagePoint's predictive indicators that
apply to a wide range of strategies.

CROSSOVERS

When a predicted moving average or other predictive indicator line for
one time period crosses above or below the moving average or other
indicator line for another time period, it suggests a trend change. This
is true for a number of different trading strategies familiar to most
traders. The advantage of VantagePoint is that crossovers that utilize
predictive indicators often provide an indication of a trend reversal

before typical moving averages and other lagging indicators; thereby, you have an early warning about direction changes.

The crossovers may involve a shorter-term predictive exponential moving average with a longer-term predictive exponential moving average, or they may involve a predictive exponential moving average crossover with an actual simple moving average.

In addition, the diverging (widening) or converging (narrowing) of two indicator lines can be used as a sign of a price move's strength or weakness and can provide evidence to support adding to or reducing the size of a market position. When the difference between two downward sloping lines on a chart reaches a maximum negative value and starts to narrow, for example, it indicates that the downward trend is beginning to lose strength and provides an early warning that the market is likely to make a bottom and turn up soon.

RISING OR FALLING NUMBERS

Forecasted moving averages and other leading technical indicators can give you valuable information by just looking at the changes in their values on VantagePoint's Daily Report or History Report without referring to a chart. When VantagePoint's forecasted moving average for a future date is greater than today's actual moving average, for example, the market is expected to move higher over that time frame. Similarly, when the forecasted moving average is less than today's actual moving average, the market is expected to move lower. The averages are updated with each new data download so the difference between the two moving averages from one time period to the next indicates the relative strength of the expected move over that time frame.

For those who prefer to look at the indicators on a chart, the slope of the indicator line provides important clues. An indicator line that is pointed up indicates strength and higher prices; an indicator line sloping downward indicates weakness and lower prices. The steepness of the line's slope suggests the degree of strength or weakness of the trend.

The same conclusions can be applied to traditional moving averages and other lagging indicators based on single-market analysis; but, the advantage of leading predictive indicators is that these changes in indicator direction and the slope of the rising/falling lines often are evident a day or two before they are noticeable on a "traditional" chart. Traders can develop a number of different strategies based on this observation alone, with their responses to this information depending on how aggressive they want to be in their trading.

The numbers for the Predicted Neural Index, as described in the previous chapter, do not get larger or smaller but alternate between a numerical value of 1.00 or 0.00. A Neural Index of 1.00 indicates that the trend direction is expected to be higher over the next two days. A Neural Index of 0.00 indicates that the trend direction is expected to be lower over the next two days.

Because VantagePoint's neural networks have been developed and trained independently for each target market, Daily Reports from other target markets can be used for additional confirmation. The Neural Index can be used as a first alert that leads to further analysis or as a filter to confirm what other indicators might be suggesting, depending on where you want to start your analysis.

BREAKOUT STRATEGIES

A basic component of a number of strategies that attempt to capitalize on breakout moves involves a crossover of the predicted moving average above or below an actual moving average. When the predicted moving average line (shown as a gray line on Figure 8.1) crosses above the actual moving average (typically shown as a black line), the market is expected to trend up. When the predicted moving average line crosses below the actual moving average line, the market is expected to trend down.

FIGURE 8.1 - BASIC CROSSOVER STRATEGY

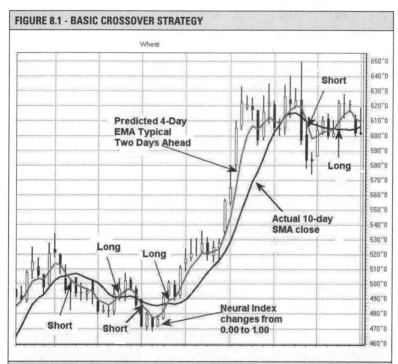

Wheat

Buying when the predicted 4-day EMA typical 2 days ahead (P4EMA+2) (gray line) crosses above the actual 10-day SMA close (A10SMA) (black line) and selling when the predicted EMA gray line crosses below the actual moving average black line got you into positions several days ahead of the turns in the actual moving average. More aggressive traders might enter positions at the first turn of the predicted moving average rather than wait for a crossover. Note that the candlesticks on the crossovers generally supported each turn – the bigger black candles (close lower than the open) on the downside crossovers and the bigger white candles (close higher than the open) on the upside crossovers.

VANTAGEPOINT INTERMARKET ANALYSIS SOFTWARE

With the six different time frames for predicted moving averages and three actual simple moving averages mentioned in the previous chapter available, VantagePoint provides a number of choices for mixing and matching moving averages of different lengths, from short-term to medium-term to long-term, depending on how sensitive you want these predictive crossover indicators to be.

One implicit assumption with this type of strategy—as with most of the trend-forecasting strategies developed with VantagePoint—is that the reading of the Neural Index should be in agreement with the trend you plan to trade, as shown on the Figure 8.1 chart (arrow) and the circled area on the Daily Report. (See Figure 8.2)

In addition to observing a crossover indicator on a VantagePoint chart, you can also see the trend changes reflected in the numbers in the predicted short-term, predicted medium-term, and predicted long-term difference columns in the Daily Report. The difference numbers compare a predicted moving average against an actual moving average, and the direction of change in the numbers indicates market strength or weakness during the time period indicated.

For a bullish indication, numbers in the predicted short-term, medium-term, and long-term difference columns on the Daily Report turn from red (minus signs) to black (positive) or they are significantly strengthening—that is, black numbers are getting larger or red numbers are getting smaller. (See Figure 8.3) As you might expect, the short-term difference numbers usually tend to turn first and bounce back and forth more, followed by the medium-term and long-term difference numbers.

When the various predicted moving average lines—or a large share of them—on the price chart have crossed the shorter moving average lines and point in the same direction and at about the same slope and the predicted short-term, medium-term, and long-term difference lines

FIGURE 8.2 - SHIFT OF THE NEURAL INDEX FROM 0.00 TO 1.00

ACTUAL MARKET DATA

Open	High	Low	Close
502^6	504^2	495^0	496^6
496^6	498^6	483^2	485^4
489^0	490^2	470^4	471^2
471^2	481^0	468^4	479^4
478^0	478^2	468^0	471^0
471^2	479^0	471^0	476^4
476^6	493^4	475^6	491^0
492^0	502^4	489^2	501^0

VANTAGEPOINT FORECASTS

Predicted Neural Index	Predicted Next Day High	Predicted Next Day Low	Predicted Short Term Difference	Predicted Medium Term Difference	Predicted Long Term Difference
0.00	505^2	491^2	4^3	5^3	-0^3
0.00	490^0	481^7	-4^5	2^0	-0^6
0.00	479^3	471^3	-11^0	-2^3	-2^7
0.00	484^3	473^2	-7^6	-4^2	-4^4
0.00	475^7	466^0	-7^0	-8^1	-6^4
1.00	482^3	473^2	-0^4	-7^2	-6^0
1.00	494^5	481^5	7^0	-4^2	-3^4
1.00	505^7	496^0	11^6	2^1	1^0

VANTAGEPOINT INTERMARKET ANALYSIS SOFTWARE

(See Figure 8.5) point in the same direction at a similar slope, it reinforces support for a price move in that direction. Your goal naturally is to use those sloping lines to catch a trend early. Once you are in the trade, it becomes a matter of trade management to determine where and when to exit. Of course, other indicators and chart patterns should point in the same direction to support your decision.

FIGURE 8.3 - SHIFT IN NUMBERS—BULLISH

ACTUAL MARKET DATA

Open	High	Low	Close
502^6	504^2	495^0	496^6
496^6	498^6	483^2	485^4
489^0	490^2	470^4	471^2
471^2	481^0	468^4	479^4
478^0	478^2	468^0	471^0
471^2	479^0	471^0	476^4
476^6	493^4	475^6	491^0
492^0	502^4	489^2	501^0

VANTAGEPOINT FORECASTS

Predicted Neural Index	Predicted Next Day High	Predicted Next Day Low	Predicted Short Term Difference	Predicted Medium Term Difference	Predicted Long Term Difference
0.00	505^2	491^2	4^3	5^3	-0^3
0.00	490^0	481^7	-4^5	2^0	-0^6
0.00	479^3	471^3	-11^0	-2^3	-2^7
0.00	484^3	473^2	-7^6	-4^2	-4^4
0.00	475^7	466^0	-7^0	-8^1	-6^4
1.00	482^3	473^2	-0^4	-7^2	-6^0
1.00	494^5	481^5	7^0	-4^2	-3^4
1.00	505^7	496^0	11^6	2^1	1^0

*Note: The shift in the predicted differences corresponds with a shift in the Neural Index from 0.00 to 1.00.

VANTAGEPOINT INTERMARKET ANALYSIS SOFTWARE

For a bearish indication, numbers in the predicted short-term, medium-term, and long-term difference columns on the Daily Report turn from black (positive) to red (minus signs) or they are significantly weakening—that is, black numbers are getting smaller or red numbers are getting larger. (See Figure 8.4) Again, the shift tends to be evident first in the short-term difference column, then in the medium-term and long-term difference columns.

FIGURE 8.4 - SHIFT IN NUMBERS—BEARISH

ACTUAL MARKET DATA

Open	High	Low	Close
675.4	685.2	674.5	684.4
684.2	693.2	682.6	689.7
691.0	693.3	689.0	690.4
690.9	691.3	684.1	687.4
687.1	688.9	677.5	682.5
682.2	683.2	665.9	667.0
667.6	674.3	666.3	672.3

VANTAGEPOINT FORECASTS

Predicted Neural Index	Predicted Next Day High	Predicted Next Day Low	Predicted Short Term Difference	Predicted Medium Term Difference	Predicted Long Term Difference
1.00	687.1	678.9	0.9	-4.1	-5.6
1.00	695.1	686.9	5.5	0.9	-2.7
1.00	696.8	690.0	7.4	4.3	0.0
0.00	692.9	680.5	2.8	3.5	0.1
0.00	688.0	677.1	-2.5	1.8	-0.5
0.00	674.6	667.2	-8.9	-2.8	-3.4
0.00	676.8	669.4	-6.5	-4.3	-3.8

*Note: The shift in the predicted differences corresponds with a shift in the Neural Index from 0.00 to 1.00.

VANTAGEPOINT INTERMARKET ANALYSIS SOFTWARE

The predicted difference indicators can also be displayed as lines on a VantagePoint chart. (See Figure 8.5) The slope or angle of the predicted difference indicator line should be the same as the comparable predicted exponential moving average for the same time frame to confirm the crossover indication. If the indicator lines do not line up closely, you may want to consider passing on the trade, even if there was a fresh crossover of the predicted moving average trend line above or below the actual moving average trend line. The more lines that are in agreement, the more solid the indication, but keep in mind that

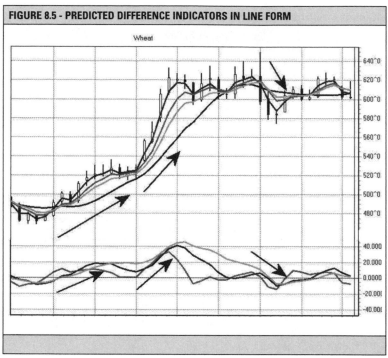

FIGURE 8.5 - PREDICTED DIFFERENCE INDICATORS IN LINE FORM

Wheat

VANTAGEPOINT INTERMARKET ANALYSIS SOFTWARE

waiting for the perfect time to place an order may mean you could be passing up good trading opportunities.

Of course, you can use these trend-forecasting strategies with multiple-contract positions to enhance your profit potential, increasing or decreasing the number of contracts or shares if the difference between two lines or numbers widens or narrows, or if the predictive indicators suggest more or less strength in the market.

Overall money management, including position sizing, is probably one of the most important factors in real trading success, and gauging the strength or weakness of a trend by observing the size of the gap between two indicator lines or the growing or declining numbers pro-

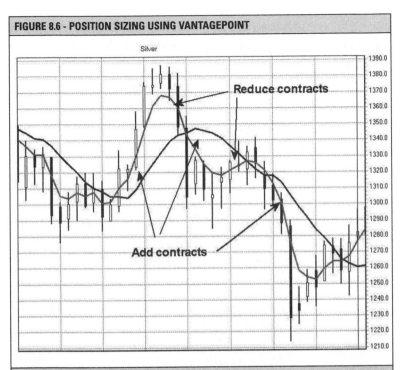

FIGURE 8.6 - POSITION SIZING USING VANTAGEPOINT

*Note how the black and white candlesticks corroborate the changing spreads in the moving averages. Building larger positions naturally entails more risk, so you will need to use sound money management techniques.

VANTAGEPOINT INTERMARKET ANALYSIS SOFTWARE

vides a mechanism for adjusting the size of positions to match what the market is telling you about the trend. Figure 8.6 shows an approach to position sizing that adds more contracts as the spread between the predicted 4-day EMA Typical two days ahead (P4EMA+2) and actual 10-day SMA close (A10SMA) widens and reduces the number of contracts as the spread between the two moving averages narrows.

MOMENTUM TRADING STRATEGIES

While market conditions sometimes favor breakouts, in which the trend direction abruptly changes, at other times the market bounces back from some price barrier or makes momentum swings back and forth within a trending or sideways range. VantagePoint predictive indicators can give you an early reading on what kind of price action to expect. Once you have identified the climate surrounding the market, the expected price direction, and the market's strength or weakness using the Neural Index, predicted crossover, and predicted difference indicators, you may conclude that the market is likely to stay within certain boundaries.

Depending on the style of trading and time frame you prefer, you can use the next day's predicted high and predicted low to set your entry and exit points. These price forecasts create the probable boundaries for the expected trading range the next day.

This is analogous to extending support and resistance lines in traditional single-market technical analysis approaches. The advantage that VantagePoint offers, though, is that the next day's high and low forecasts, based on the pattern recognition capabilities of neural networks applied to intermarket data, are determined objectively and are not just an arbitrary linear extrapolation from past single-market data.

This information can be used like pivot points or support/resistance areas against which to trade, based on the premise that prices will generally stay within the day's predicted range. Or, it can be used to determine where to place stops to enter or exit the market if prices move outside the predicted range.

A market that is advancing will usually not touch the line denoting the predicted lows, for example, making a point below the next day's predicted low a good spot for a stop on a long position if the market does not continue to make the expected upward move. If a market that has been rising does tumble below the next day's predicted low, it's a sign that the market has turned weaker and may be set up for a trend reversal to the downside.

If you are a day trader, you can use the forecasts of the next day's high and low to identify low-risk day trades. If the Neural Index and forecasted moving average indicators for a specific target market indicate that the next day is expected to be a down day, you can wait for the market to trade up toward the predicted high before initiating a short position with a limit or market order, with the intention of closing out the trade near the predicted low.

Similarly, long positions can be entered near the predicted low on a day the market is expected to move up, with exits near the predicted high.

You may place your limit order a specific number of ticks below the predicted high or above the predicted low for either entry or exit, or you may use a percentage of the day's expected range to determine how far below the predicted high or above the predicted low your order should be. For example, the distance may be 20% of the day's predicted range. For forex, the distance might be 15-20 pips inside the predicted low or predicted high. This is a judgment call and may vary with your experience with different markets.

If the current trend is up, you could place a limit buy order a specified distance above the predicted low and set a protective stop several ticks below the predicted low or at a logical chart point that is within your risk tolerance level. If the current trend is down, you could place a limit order to sell at a specified distance below the predicted high and set a protective stop several ticks above the predicted high or at a logical chart point that is within your risk tolerance level.

To exit a trade after you get into a position with your limit order, you might set a profit target that is about 80% of the day's predicted trading range, placing another limit order to exit the position. In essence, you

FIGURE 8.7 - DAILY REPORT SHOWING SIGNS OF A DOWNTRENDING MARKET

VANTAGEPOINT FORECASTS

Predicted Neural Index	Predicted Next Day High	Predicted Next Day Low	Predicted Short Term Difference	Predicted Medium Term Difference	Predicted Long Term Difference
1.00	112^15	111^17	0^04	0^04	0^05
0.00	112^06	111^04	0^00	0^05	0^04
0.00	111^21	110^23	-0^08	0^00	0^00
1.00	111^29	111^08	-0^05	-0^01	0^00
0.00	111^23	110^30	-0^06	-0^05	-0^01
0.00	111^14	110^17	-0^08	-0^09	-0^04
0.00	111^06	110^20	-0^07	-0^11	-0^07
0.00	111^10	110^19	-0^05	-0^11	-0^08
0.00	110^26	110^00	-0^10	-0^16	-0^13
0.00	110^10	109^13	-0^16	-0^22	-0^21
0.00	110^13	109^23	-0^11	-0^21	-0^23
0.00	109^31	109^07	-0^13	-0^22	-0^27
0.00	109^18	108^28	-0^14	-0^26	-0^31
0.00	109^23	109^00	-0^08	-0^23	-1^00
0.00	109^22	108^28	-0^05	-0^20	-0^31

VANTAGEPOINT INTERMARKET ANALYSIS SOFTWARE

are only attempting to fade the day's predicted high or low, assuming that the market will bounce back into the expected range after trading near the predicted high or low.

Note: You may not get into or out of a position with a limit order so you may have to use some discretion on entries/exits. With this type of trade, you take what the market gives you during the day and do not attempt to hold for a long-term trade that can put you at risk overnight or over a weekend.

This tactic allows day traders to sell rallies within an expected downtrend or buy dips within an expected uptrend one or more times daily,

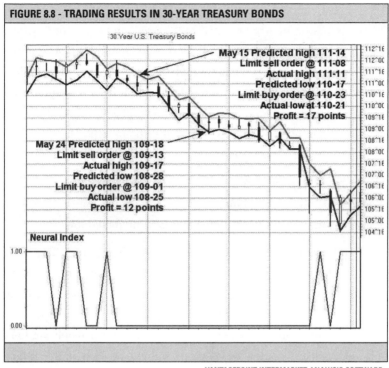

FIGURE 8.8 - TRADING RESULTS IN 30-YEAR TREASURY BONDS

30 Year U.S. Treasury Bonds

May 15 Predicted high 111-14
Limit sell order @ 111-08
Actual high 111-11
Predicted low 110-17
Limit buy order @ 110-23
Actual low at 110-21
Profit = 17 points

May 24 Predicted high 109-18
Limit sell order @ 109-13
Actual high 109-17
Predicted low 108-28
Limit buy order @ 109-01
Actual low 108-25
Profit = 12 points

Neural Index

VANTAGEPOINT INTERMARKET ANALYSIS SOFTWARE

depending on the intraday market volatility. Although some traders day trade against the prevailing trend, day trading in the direction of the prevailing trend is generally a better choice for this strategy because in a downtrend, the market is more likely to be near its predicted high early in the trading session and to close near its daily low and the predicted low. In an uptrend, the market is likely to trade near its low early and then close near the day's high and predicted high. The profitability of day trades that are executed with this strategy can be substantial with minimal risk because tight stops can be utilized.

Figure 8.7 and Figure 8.8 illustrate one of these intraday trades in T-bond futures. On May 14 the predicted high for the next day, May

15, is 111-14 and the predicted low is 110-17 (underlined), a range of 29 points. Using an arbitrary 20% of the predicted range, or 6 points, for the placement of orders, a sell limit order would be placed at the predicted high minus 6 points or 111-08. If filled, two other orders could be placed, one a limit buy order 6 points above the predicted low or 110-23 and the other a protective buy stop 6 points above the predicted high at 111-20 (or at some other point depending on chart patterns and risk management).

The same strategy also worked well on May 24 when May 23 data (underlined) predicted a range of 22 points; so, the limit orders were placed 5 points from the predicted high and predicted low.

Figure 8.8 illustrates the results of this day-trading strategy. This trade works best with markets that have a wide enough daily range to allow for sufficient profits because the trade is not designed to capture the whole range. It is also important to recognize that such a trade may not be executed every day because prices may never reach the limit sell order price. Also, the trade entry should come early in the trading session to give the market time to move. In some cases, a trader might put a sell stop at a specified distance below the predicted low in case prices drop, which would be a sign of real weakness, such as occurred in June on this chart.

Position traders can use VantagePoint's predicted highs and lows to set entry points and then as a guide to move stops as the market moves. Day traders can use the same predicted highs and lows for intraday trading. If other indicators suggest tomorrow will be an up day, they can wait for the market to trade down toward the predicted low and place a limit order several ticks above the predicted low to get into a long position, closing it out as prices approach the day's predicted high.

A position trader can use the same forecasts of the next day's high and low to enter positions with a breakout strategy, then use the subsequent days' forecasts to move stops or exit the trade. For example, if the market has been in a downtrend but the predictive indicators are pointing to a reversal to an uptrend, you could put a buy stop somewhere above the predicted high for the next day. The exact spot will depend on your risk propensity, but your stop should be sufficiently above VantagePoint's predicted high for the next day to lessen the probability of getting into a position prematurely due to intraday market volatility.

When prices make a sharp jump outside of their predicted range, it suggests a strong move in the direction of the breakout, which could continue enough to make a long position profitable. As protection, a sell stop could be placed below the predicted low or at a logical chart point in case there is no follow through on the upside breakout.

In a strong uptrend, the daily price ranges are noticeably above the predicted lows, and the market tends to close well above the predicted high, as the white candlesticks on Figure 8.9 illustrate. In a strong downtrend, the daily ranges tend to stay below the predicted highs, and the market tends to close well below the predicted low, as the black candlesticks confirm. When a market open or low is above the predicted high, it is a particularly strong buy indication, especially in conjunction with a bullish chart pattern such as exceeding a previous high, which occurred on June 11 on Figure 8.9.

The same type of tactic applies to placing stops on a position you already hold. For example, if you are short, place your buy stop far enough above the predicted high to reduce the chances of getting taken out of your position prematurely, yet close enough to protect you in the event the market penetrates the predicted high and breaks out

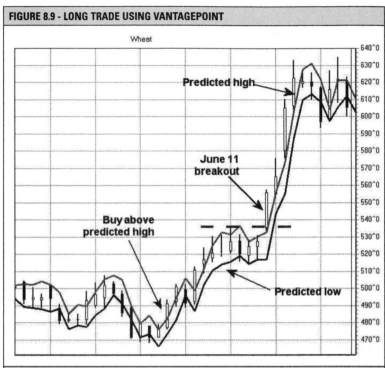

FIGURE 8.9 - LONG TRADE USING VANTAGEPOINT

Wheat

Predicted high

June 11
breakout

Buy above
predicted high

Predicted low

By placing a buy stop at some distance above the next day's predicted high, it's possible
to get into a long position as the market breaks out of the upside of the predicted daily
range and continues to move sharply higher.

VANTAGEPOINT INTERMARKET ANALYSIS SOFTWARE

to the upside. The benefit of setting your stop based on forecasts of the
next day's high or low is that your stop is less likely to be clustered
among other traders' stops, which are often set using traditional methods of single-market analysis.

In any case, do not place a stop loss within the forecasted trading range.
Review the VantagePoint forecasts every night and adjust your stops. If
you're long, you can put your sell stop below the predicted low; if you're
short, you can put your buy stop above the predicted high.

Once a position has built up profits, you may want to use tight trailing stops instead of stationary stops, or you may want to maintain your open position until the market hits a predetermined profit target that you specify. Keep in mind that markets often move up and down, even within trends, and do not tend to make extended moves in one direction; therefore, it may be wise to set a price target as some momentum strategies prescribe. When a profit target has been reached, you can exit the position "at the market" or, if you are feeling more aggressive, you can move your stop nearer the target. This way, if the market does retrace, you're stopped out for approximately your target amount but, if the market keeps running, you'll pick up additional profits.

By studying the market you are trading, you will become familiar with its characteristics to determine how far it is likely to "run" or where it is likely to reverse, based on chart analysis of past price action.

Another strategy based on trading against a boundary involves using a moving average as the boundary. Figure 8.10 is basically the same chart as Figure 8.1, which we used to illustrate a predicted crossover indicator. However instead of being concerned about a break below the moving average and trend line and where to place a stop to protect profits, a trader sensing a strong market could use the dip in early June as a place for a limit buy order as the market returns to the vicinity of the moving average "boundary."

Assuming prices would rebound from support provided by VantagePoint's Predicted 8-day EMA Typical Two Days Ahead and resume the uptrend, the trader might add on to an existing position or establish a new long position in the vicinity of the moving average. A protective sell stop could be placed below the lows to reduce the risk. By waiting for the June 11 breakout higher to jump onboard the uptrend with a buy stop order, as suggested in Figure 8.9, the trader

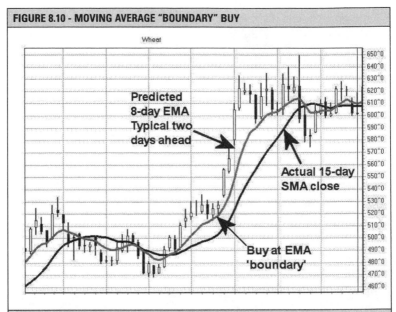

FIGURE 8.10 - MOVING AVERAGE "BOUNDARY" BUY

Wheat

Predicted
8-day EMA
Typical two
days ahead

Actual 15-day
SMA close

Buy at EMA
'boundary'

If you got into a long position in wheat futures on a VantagePoint predictive crossover indicator in late May, you are still in a good position by staying with the trend on the dip in early June. But if you missed the crossover signal or want to add to your position, the setback to "support" at the moving average line provides another place to buy.

VANTAGEPOINT INTERMARKET ANALYSIS SOFTWARE

might have experienced some severe slippage as the market gapped up and closed sharply higher that day.

Even when markets are trending, they often have small setbacks toward a moving average or trend line. These are the flags and pennants described in the chapter on chart patterns. It is important to analyze the candlesticks and to have a good sense of the market's fundamentals as prices approach these key areas so you can see how other traders are reacting to the latest developments. In some cases, after spotting a test of a moving average line like the one on the daily wheat chart, you may want to shift to intraday charts to implement a trading strategy with more precise order placement.

Which moving average works best with this strategy? The answer will require you to study VantagePoint's predictive moving averages and to experiment with different markets to determine what will work most effectively for each market, given your own trading objectives, risk propensity, and amount of trading capital available.

MOMENTUM INDICATOR STRATEGIES

VantagePoint's predictive momentum indicators—Moving Average Convergence-Divergence (MACD), Relative Strength Index (RSI), True Strength Index (TSI), and stochastics—can also be incorporated into a number of trading strategies. In fact, in a trending market situation, it may be a good idea to look at a momentum oscillator, such as predictive stochastics or RSI. These are most useful in choppy market conditions; therefore, you can get a different perspective on price action because you never know when a market may change from trending to choppy or vice versa.

VantagePoint predicts the values of these momentum indicators one day ahead to help you get an early reading on an overbought or oversold condition that may not have become evident to other traders using traditional momentum indicators.

Figure 8.11 shows just one example of how stochastics may be utilized with other VantagePoint predictive indicators in a trading strategy:

- Enter at the close when the predicted medium-term difference crosses the zero line in the direction of the trade and when predicted stochastics is between 30 and 60 for a long position or between 40 and 70 for a short position.

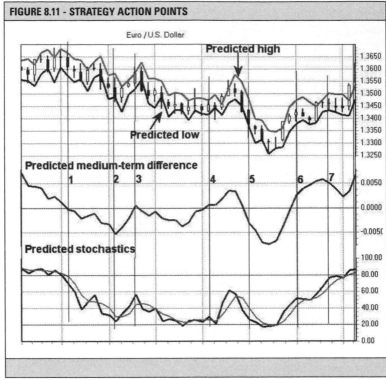

FIGURE 8.11 - STRATEGY ACTION POINTS

Euro / U.S. Dollar

VANTAGEPOINT INTERMARKET ANALYSIS SOFTWARE

- Set and reset the stop loss daily near the predicted next day high or predicted next day low, whichever is applicable.

- Exit at the close when the predicted stochastic moves above 70 for a long position or below 30 for a short position or when either the predicted next day high or the predicted next day low suggests that the trade should be closed.

This strategy requires a trending indicator and a momentum indicator to be on the same wave length, so there may be fewer trade opportunities than with some other strategies. Here is the situation at each of the numbers on the chart:

1. Predicted medium-term difference (PTMDiff) drops below zero line, predicted stochastics (PStoch) just below 70 threshold, you sell on close at 1.3607.

2. Depending on how tightly you place a protective buy stop to the predicted highs, you might have been stopped out at 1.3597 three days after you entered; but, assuming you remained short, you would exit at the close at 1.3483 when PStoch falls below 30.

3. PTMDiff edges above the zero line with PStoch at 56, meaning a long position at the close at 1.3586, but you are stopped out of the long position the next day when the market falls well below the predicted low at 1.3557.

4. PTMDiff moves above the zero line, suggesting a long position, but PStoch is below the minimum threshold of 30 so there is no long trade.

5. PTMDiff plummets below the zero line but PStoch is already below 30 so there is no short trade.

6. PTMDiff surges above the zero line with PStoch at 52, indicating a long trade at the close at 1.3425.

7. PStoch moves above 70, requiring you to exit the long position at the close at 1.3458.

Could this strategy be refined to take trades right after PTMDiff turns up or down or could you use some other exit tactic so you remain in a trade longer than the 30-70 PStoch boundaries allow? Probably. Any strategy is open for more research and tweaking.

Although momentum indicators can be useful in spotting underlying market strength or weakness, they do have some shortcomings and should be used in conjunction with other indicators or approaches. They may remain in a buy or sell zone for days or weeks, giving false clues about a market reversal while prices continue to trend higher or lower for extended periods.

TRADING WITH OPTIONS

Instead of buying stocks, futures contracts, or cash currencies, you can use predictive indicators to position yourself in options. This alternative opens up another whole new set of trading strategies based on the market direction forecasted by intermarket analysis.

There is a lot more to options than simply buying calls when the indications are bullish or buying puts when the indications are bearish. You need to understand the intricacies of various option trading strategies (including option spreading) in order to take advantage of trending markets or markets that are channeling between support and resistance.

If you do decide to trade options, you should be familiar with their characteristics, a subject well beyond the scope of this book, and one that requires its own book or course of study.

STRATEGIES: FINAL WORDS

This is certainly not an exhaustive list of possible strategies using intermarket data and predictive indicators. In effect, these are only offered as suggested strategies for your consideration and from which to develop other strategies. Your only limitations on developing strategies are your imagination and the time you have to do the research on how the various indicators perform under various trading conditions.

As has been mentioned before, any trading or analysis that you do with strategies developed from intermarket data should be done in conjunction with your experience in reading chart patterns (including candlestick formations), as well as whatever other indicators—even single-market, trend-following ones—with which you are already familiar. And keep one eye on fundamentals and outside events that can produce market shocks that no trading strategy can foresee.

Also, as part of your intermarket analysis, keep track of what the indicators are saying about the markets closely related to the target market you are trading. The Eurodollar, 2-year Treasury notes, 5-year Treasury notes, and 30-year Treasury bonds, for example, add considerable insight into what is likely to happen to 10-year Treasury notes because these five markets taken together encompass the entire interest rate yield curve from 90 days to 30 years. The more the forecasted indicators on these other related reports confirm the indicators on the 10-year Treasury notes, the higher the probability that the 10-year Treasury note market will act as expected. Similarly, if you are trading crude oil, you need to recognize that this market does not trade in a vacuum, so you should be paying close attention to other related markets including others in the oil complex, the U.S. dollar, gold, etc.

This way, if reports from these related markets give contrary indications, you should be more cautious. Similar confirmations or divergences can be found among the stock sectors and indexes, currencies, and many other commodities. Remember, no market trades in isolation in today's global financial system. They are all related, and to be successful, your trading strategies and analyses need to reflect that fact.

Chapter 9

THE SYNERGISTIC TRADER

As the world's financial markets have become increasingly integrated, intermarket analysis now plays a crucial role in analyzing and trading today's global markets, just as back-testing and optimization of single-market trading strategies became integral to computerized technical analysis in the 1980s.

But successful market analysis means more than just intermarket analysis, as has been pointed out previously in this book. Traders have to look at today's markets from a three-dimensional perspective. In the late 1980s I first wrote about this concept, which I call "Synergistic Market Analysis." It is a method that combines single-market technical analysis, intermarket analysis, and fundamental analysis. In effect, it looks at financial market analysis as a three-legged stool in which all three perspectives offer their own unique insight into market dynamics.

Interestingly, due to their robust nature, neural networks are well-suited for analyzing markets from both a single-market and an intermarket perspective and for incorporating fundamental data inputs. These might include the latest supply and demand statistics or economic data, such as the Gross Domestic Product, Producer Price Index, Consumer Price Index, or employment statistics. Even comparative economic statistics from different countries can be included.

> As the interrelationships of the global financial markets continue to evolve and become even more complex and fast-paced, technical analysis, intermarket analysis, and fundamental analysis will need to become blended together.

In effect, as the interrelationships of the global financial markets continue to evolve and become even more complex and fast-paced, technical analysis, intermarket analysis, and fundamental analysis will need to become blended together. Utilizing the computational modeling capabilities of neural networks in a structured framework integrates seemingly disparate technical, intermarket, and fundamental data. In this way the trader gains innovative, quantitative trend forecasting indicators that can be developed and tested, and this will keep them at the cutting edge of financial market analysis for the foreseeable future.

ACCEPTING TECHNOLOGICAL ADVANCES

History is replete with stories about newly emerging technologies that have subsequently had a major impact on economic development and the financial markets. The railroad, the airplane, the telephone, xerography, personal computers, and the Internet represent such technologies that had substantial commercial applications and became part of the economic and social landscape. Yet, at first they were received with some degree of skepticism because it is always more comfortable to maintain the status quo.

But technological progress cannot be held back by those who are skeptical, inflexible, or simply too insecure to adopt something new or different. Such close-mindedness and shortsightedness is a dangerous anachronistic trait to have in such a rapidly changing, technology-driven, darwinistic, global economy.

Within the financial industry, the same can be said for the application of advanced quantitative technologies such as neural networks and intermarket analysis to global financial market analysis and trading. In the past, analytical innovations involving the application of quantitative technologies have, strangely enough, often met strong resistance within the financial industry. In the future, though, as new technologies are developed and can demonstrate their effectiveness, they will become incorporated into the practice of financial market analysis much more quickly.

Neural networks have proven they work in many different applications including intermarket analysis, and they are here to stay. Still, they are just one of many potential mathematical tools that can be applied to implementing synergistic trading strategies. Other technologies—expert systems, genetic algorithms, fractal geometry, chaos theory, and fuzzy logic, to name a few—are also being applied to market analysis with varying degrees of success. There is certainly much more research needed.

It really shouldn't need to be said, though, that there will never be a foolproof way to forecast the markets, no matter what approach or technique is used. A financial crystal ball simply does not exist despite what some promotional and marketing materials suggest. If that is what you are looking for, you will be very disappointed.

In my opinion, it's not possible to be able to predict future prices and trend direction with more than maybe 85% accuracy, due to inherent randomness and unpredictable outside events that will continue to affect the global financial markets, as well as the sheer difficulty of developing and implementing effective forecasting tools. Even if that level is approached on a market-wide basis, a myriad of additional factors, not the least of which include indecisive decision making, lack of trading experience, and the psychology of fear and greed, all affect individual trading performance and can turn what otherwise might have been a winning trade into a loser. In this case, there is no one to blame but the trader himself.

MAINTAINING THE PUSH FOR ACCURACY

As a youthful sixty-year old now, I want to continue to be involved in pushing the forecasting envelope as far as it will go in the application of personal computers to the financial markets. It's been my passion most of my adult life. This challenge is what has made the financial markets and technical analysis so exciting and intellectually stimulating to me—even more so than trading itself. My research and development efforts, which began in earnest in the late 1970s, will continue to be focused on improving forecasting accuracy through whatever means possible.

I hope that this book has helped make you more aware of the implications that the globalization of the financial markets has on your own trading. I am confident that by broadening your perspective to include intermarket analysis (and eventually by blending single-market analysis, intermarket analysis, and fundamental analysis), whether you are a stock, options, futures, or forex trader, you will be able to improve your trading performance and increase your self-confidence to make more decisive and well-thought-through trading decisions. And, you will have more fun doing it.

TRADING RESOURCE GUIDE

SUGGESTED READING

THE VISUAL INVESTOR: HOW TO SPOT MARKET TRENDS
by John Murphy

It's technical analysis made easy! This bestseller shows how to track the ups and downs of stock prices by visually comparing charts - instead of relying on complex formulas and technical concepts. Includes software demo disks, step-by-step instructions for using charts & graphs, and more.

$65.00   ITEM #2379

INTERMARKET ANALYSIS: PROFITING FROM GLOBAL MARKET RELATIONSHIPS
by John Murphy

John Murphy on Intermarket Analysis updates the groundbreaking work of a well-known and highly respected technical analyst. A leading educator, Murphy walks the reader through his key tools to understanding global markets and shows investors where they can profit, bull or bear market.

$80.00   ITEM #1523697

FOREX TRADING USING INTERMARKET ANALYSIS: DISCOVERING HIDDEN MARKET RELATIONSHIPS THAT PROVIDE EARLY CLUES FOR PRICE DIRECTION
by Louis Mendelsohn

In today's global marketplace, currency values fluctuate every day and foreign exchange is the biggest market of them all, trading well over $1 trillion a day—more than all other markets combined! Master this market that never sleeps, and you could be the big winner. Just to survive in the hottest marketplace in the world, you will have to learn to stay one step ahead of the game.

$19.99   ITEM #4183039

TECHNICAL ANALYSIS OF THE FINANCIAL MARKETS
by John Murphy

From how to read charts to understanding indicators and the crucial role of technical analysis in investing, you won't find a more thorough or up-to-date source. Revised and expanded for today's changing financial world, it applies to equities as well as the futures markets.

$85.00   ITEM #10239

TRADE YOUR WAY TO FINANCIAL FREEDOM
by Van K. Tharp

One of Schwager's famed "Market Wizards" answers the burning question: What's the one trading method that will bring you trading and financial success? A must read.

$34.95   ITEM #4203544

TRADING IN THE ZONE: MASTER THE MARKET WITH CONFIDENCE, DISCIPLINE AND A WINNING ATTITUDE
by Mark Douglas

Famed trading coach and "Disciplined Trader" author Mark Douglas provides 5 key steps to successful trading results. Even well grounded traders often fall victim to lapses in judgement and outside pressures that affect stock picking and trading moves. Now, find specific solutions to some of trading's most complicated issues - and learn to triumph over outside influences with the simple excercises found in Douglas' latest #1 seller.

$50.00   ITEM #11833

IMPORTANT INTERNET SITES

Traders' Library Bookstore   www.traderslibrary.com

Traders' Library, a division of Expert Trading LTD., was founded in 1991 and created as a book distribution company targeted to the full spectrum of the investment arena - from individual investors and financial advisors to professional traders.

Louis Mendelsohn   www.FutureForecasts.com

Biographical information on Louis Mendelsohn, access to his personal library of articles, speeches and book contributions arranged by subject matter.

Market Technologies, LLC   www.TraderTech.com

Headquartered in Tampa Bay since its founding in 1979 by Louis B. Mendelsohn, with trading software customers in over 90 countries worldwide, Market Technologies is a fast growing, Inc. 500, company and recognized world leader in market forecasting. Market Technologies researches and develops proprietary trend forecasting and market timing technologies that utilize artificial intelligence applied to intermarket analysis, in order to forecast global commodity and financial markets.

Trading Education.com, LLC   www.TradingEducation.com

Established in September 2005, TradingEducation.com, LLC has developed into a comprehensive internet resource offering traders free educational materials, quotes, and market relevant news for stocks, exchange-traded funds, commodities, currencies, futures and options. Traders from all experience levels can benefit from the wealth of information and tools available at TradingEducation.com which seeks to enhance their trading strategies and avoid costly mistakes.

BROKERAGES

Daniels Trading | 800.800.3840 US/Canada | 312.706.7600 Intl

www.DanielsTrading.com

Established by renowned commodity trader Andy Daniels in 1995, Daniels Trading is a fully licensed commodity futures, forex and options brokerage firm offering individual and institutional investors the option of executing their orders through a commodity broker, an automated trading system, or one of several self-directed online trading platforms. "Excellence Through Execution" is the firm's mission and by providing a diverse array of FCM clearing relationships, professional electronic execution platforms, robust automated trading systems and competitive trading costs, Daniels Trading fulfills its mission for astute futures, forex and option traders worldwide. Although trade execution is the firm's primary focus, it also places high priorities on customer education and communication.

MF Global   **www.MFGlobal.ca**

MF Global Canada is a leader in the Canadian futures and options market, leveraging its worldwide presence to deliver exceptional execution and clearing services for private, commercial and institutional clients. While a leading derivatives broker, the firm also provides unparalleled expertise in equities, alternative investments and foreign exchange trading.

Trade Center, LLC | 800. 894 8194 US/Canada | 949.643.7100 Intl

www.TradeCenterLLC.com

Founded in 1994, Trade Center is a professionally managed Independent Introducing Broker, offering clearing capabilities at Citi/Smith Barney, MF Global and R.J. O'Brien Futures. Trade Center specializes in alternative investing and asset diversification utilizing the Futures and FX global markets through the administration of trading systems and managed accounts programs. TradeCenterPro.com is the On-Line division of Trade Center, LLC, providing an easy to use order entry system, including free real time quotes and charts for futures and options markets around the globe.

EXCHANGES

Chicago Board Options Exchange   www.cboe.com

Located at 400 South LaSalle Street in Chicago, CBOE is one of the world's largest options exchanges with an annual trade of over 450 million options contracts, covering more than 1200 companies, 50 stock indexes, and 50 exchange-traded funds (ETFs). The exchange was established in 1973, when it created and listed the first exchange-listed standardized stock options.

CME Group   www.CMEGroup.com

CME Group is a combined entity formed by the 2007 merger of the Chicago Mercantile Exchange (CME) and the Chicago Board of Trade (CBOT). It provides the widest range of benchmark futures and options products available on any exchange, covering all major asset classes.

New York Mercantile Exchange   www.nymex.com

The New York Mercantile Exchange, Inc. is the world's largest physical commodity futures exchange and the preeminent trading forum for energy and precious metals. The Exchange has stood for market integrity and price transparency for more than 130 years.

New York Stock Exchange   www.nyse.com

NYSE Euronext, the holding company created by the combination of NYSE Group, Inc. and Euronext N.V., was launched on April 4, 2007. NYSE Euronext (NYSE/New York and Euronext/Paris: NYX) operates the world's largest and most liquid exchange group and offers the most diverse array of financial products and services.

NASDAQ   www.NASDAQ.com

NASDAQ is the largest U.S. electronic stock market. With approximately 3,200 companies, it lists more companies and, on average, trades more shares per day than any other U.S. market. It is home to companies that are leaders across all areas of business, including technology, retail, communications, financial services, transportation, media and biotechnology.

ABOUT THE AUTHOR
AND
MARKET TECHNOLOGIES, LLC

Louis B. Mendelsohn, President and Chief Executive Officer of Market Technologies, LLC, is a world-renowned pioneer in the application of personal computers to technical analysis and the global financial markets and is the developer of VantagePoint Intermarket Analysis Software.

Born in 1948 in Providence, Rhode Island, Mr. Mendelsohn received a B.S. degree in Administration and Management Science from Carnegie Mellon University's Tepper School of Business in 1969, a M.S.W. degree from the State University of New York at Buffalo in 1973, and a M.B.A. degree with Honors from Boston University in 1977.

Mr. Mendelsohn began trading stocks and options in the early 1970s when he was in graduate school. Then, while employed as a hospital administrator in the late 1970s, he began trading commodities, as both a day and position trader, and started writing software programs for himself and other traders to analyze the commodities markets. This led to the founding of Market Technologies in 1979. Since then, he has served as the firm's President and Chief Executive Officer, overseeing all aspects of the company's phenomenal growth.

In 1980 he left hospital administration to devote his full attention to trading and applying personal computers to technical analysis. Three years later Mr. Mendelsohn introduced ProfitTaker, the first commercially available strategy back-testing and optimization trading software for personal computers in the financial industry.

Mr. Mendelsohn was one of the first professionals in the financial industry to recognize the emerging trend toward globalization of the world's economy and financial markets in the mid-1980s and again broke new ground in the field of technical analysis when he developed Trader, the first commercially available intermarket analysis trading software for personal computers in the financial industry.

Building on his extensive research since the mid-1980s involving intermarket analysis applied to global market data and trend forecasting, in 1991 Mr. Mendelsohn released the first version of VantagePoint Intermarket Analysis Software, which uses a highly sophisticated mathematical tool known as neural networks to analyze the effects of multiple global markets on each other and make short-term market forecasts.

Since then, Mr. Mendelsohn's research has continued to focus on the global financial markets, the application of intermarket analysis to global market data, and how to use this information to make highly accurate, short-term market forecasts. Mr. Mendelsohn has written extensively since 1983 in many prominent financial publications including *Barron's*, *Futures*, and *Technical Analysis of Stocks & Commodities*. He has been widely quoted in the financial media including the *Wall Street Journal* and *Investor's Business Daily*, has collaborated with other technical analysis experts on more than half a dozen books on technical analysis, and has been interviewed live on national radio and television, including CNN, Bloomberg Television, and CNBC. Mr. Mendelsohn's first book on intermarket analysis, Trend Forecasting with Intermarket Analysis, was published in December 2000. His second book, Forex Trading Using Intermarket Analysis, was released in March 2006.

Because of his pioneering achievements in the application of personal computers to technical analysis over the past quarter-century, Mr. Mendelsohn's biography was selected for inclusion in Marquis Who's Who in the World, Who's Who in America, Who's Who in Finance and Industry, and in a time capsule at the White House in Washington, D.C. He has been a full member of the Market Technicians Association since 1988 and a colleague of the International Federation of Technical Analysts.

Mr. Mendelsohn has been invited to speak at numerous financial conferences and symposia, including the Futures Industry Association annual meeting, Futures Symposium International, the Harvard Business School Alumni Club, Futures Truth, and the annual meeting of the Association for Investment Management and Research.

Since its founding by Mr. Mendelsohn, Market Technologies has been at the forefront in the development of technical analysis trading software to assist traders in the financial markets. Located in the Tampa Bay region on Florida's west coast since 1979, the firm has customers in more than 90 countries throughout the world.

In 1999 Market Technologies was honored by then-governor Jeb Bush for its ranking as the 29th fastest growing privately-held company in Florida in the Florida 100 competition sponsored by the University of Florida, Deloitte & Touche LLP, PricewaterhouseCoopers LLP, and Raymond James & Associates, Inc.

From 1998 to 2002 Market Technologies also ranked as one of the fastest growing technology companies, both public and private, in the Tampa Bay Fast 50 competition sponsored by Deloitte & Touche LLP. In 2004 Market Technologies was recognized by Inc. magazine as one of the fastest growing privately-held companies in the United States. Well-known companies that have been selected for the Inc. 500 list of the next generation of world-class companies in the past include Microsoft, Oracle, and Morningstar.

More recently, in 2007 Market Technologies ranked as the 25th fastest growing privately-held company in the Tampa Bay Business Journal's Fast 50 competition, and was also a second-time winner in Inc. magazine's national competition of privately-held companies.

COMPANY INFORMATION:

Market Technologies, LLC

5807 Old Pasco Road

Wesley Chapel, Florida 33544

E-mail address: Global@TraderTech.com

Internet Web site address: www.TraderTech.com/Global

USA and Canada: 800-732-5407

International: 813-973-0496

Fax: 813-973-2700